Images of Jazz

Buescher

Images of Jazz

Lee Tanner

Foreword by
Nat Hentoff

FRIEDMAN/FAIRFAX
PUBLISHERS

A FRIEDMAN/FAIRFAX BOOK

Library of Congress Cataloging-in-Publication data available upon request.

ISBN 1-56799-367-2

Project Editor: Sharyn Rosart
Editor: Nathaniel Marunas
Production Editor: Loretta Mowat
Art Director/Designer: Lynne Yeamans
Photography Editor: Christopher C. Bain
Production Director: Karen Matsu Greenberg

Color separations by Bright Arts Graphics (S) Pte Ltd
Printed in China by Leefung-Asco Printers Ltd.

For bulk purchases and special sales, please contact:
Friedman/Fairfax Publishers
Attention: Sales Department
15 West 26th Street
New York, New York 10010
212/685-6610 FAX 212/685-1307

Visit the Friedman/Fairfax Website:
http://www.webcom.com/friedman

Coleman Hawkins, Symphony Hall, Boston, 1967

For all the remarkable musicians who have given us all so much of their heart and soul, and especially for Bix, Bunny, Charlie, Chu, Herschel, Jimmy, Sonny, Davey, Booker, Eric, Bud, Albert, Allen, Tiny, Tadd, Fats, Jug, Richie, Lee, Trane, Cannonball, Grant, Herbie, Bird, Prez, Paul, Bobby, Gary, Gabor, and (too) many others who only had a fraction of their lifetimes to do their thing.

And for Linda. Thank you for your love, support, and inspiration.

Acknowledgments

Special thanks to the designer and the editors: Lynne Yeamans, Sharyn Rosart, Nathaniel Marunas, Loretta Mowat, and Chris Bain for their superb handling of the material and for their patience. Thanks also to John Turner for his expert help with all things photographic, and my deep appreciation to Nat Hentoff, Gene Lees, and Ben Sidran for reviewing the text, and for their helpful comments and advice.

Finally, my deep gratitude to five dear friends, Joe Ryner, Phil Clapp, Fred Miller, Steve Flehinger, and Dick Lewis, who helped me get "The Jazz Image" off the ground.

Chet
Baker,
The Jazz
Workshop,
Boston,
1966

Contents

Roy Eldridge,
Connolly's,
Boston, 1958

Foreword

Music is your own experience, your thoughts and your wisdom.
If you don't live it, it won't come out of your horn.

—Charlie Parker

There have been a number of compelling jazz photographers through the decades, but only a few have gone deeper than the decisive musical moment to the essence of the improviser—his life off as well as on the stand. Of those few, Lee Tanner is the most consistent in his ability to find the person at the core of the player.

For instance, I knew Red Allen for many years, and Tanner's 1958 photograph of him best distills Red's pride in his knowledge of how influential he was. Miles Davis, for one, told me at that time Red had been taking creative risks that helped shape younger players. Yet Red was very shy off the stand, and he often showboated on the stand. But this photograph, more than any other of Red, shows that he knew his worth—and so did Lee Tanner.

Also penetrating is the 1968 picture of Thelonious Monk. On the one hand, no one in jazz was more adventurous and stubbornly original than Monk. On the other hand, away from music, he was very vulnerable—dependent on his wife, Nellie, for a saving order in his life. And he was sometimes afraid of the unfamiliar in the world outside. You can feel Monk's vulnerability in Lee's photograph.

There is the world-famous 1962 Tanner photograph of Duke Ellington. Duke was masterful not only in his composition and the direction of his orchestra but also in slkily masking his feelings and intentions. It took me years to get him to talk about his angers, his hopes, his frustrations. In this photograph, you see the private Ellington way beneath "I Love You Madly."

Coleman Hawkins spent much of his life on the road. When he'd come to town, the young local tenors would be waiting to challenge him. For many years, he was king of the road—with a sound and ideas so powerful that they could blow you off the stand. Musicians called him the "Bean" because he had so much in his head. Tanner's 1958 photograph of Hawkins wisely shows him without a horn in his mouth. Instead, you see why, when Bean came into a studio or a club, he commanded the room—because he was so magisterial.

"Little" Jimmy Rushing got inside the lyrics of the blues and ballads in a way that sounded as if he were telling you some of his more intimate memories, thereby bringing to light some of your own long-hidden desires and disappointments. Rushing was a gentle, indeed tender, man, and those are qualities that have been forever recorded in Lee's 1966 picture.

If I had to choose the one musician who most resoundingly exemplifies the joy of jazz, it would be Roy Eldridge. He was also the fiercest competitor in jazz that I have ever heard. Roy never coasted. I watched him for a week as we prepared the TV program *The Sound of Jazz* on CBS in 1957. Before we actually went on the air, there were lighting sessions and sound checks and during each of them Roy played as if his entire reputation depended on each solo he took—even though no one was listening but the technicians and the other musicians. That sheer pleasure in continually challenging himself is clear in Tanner's 1958 photo of Roy.

In all of his photographs, Lee Tanner makes vivid the sheer energy of jazz—the life force. Especially invigorating is Lee's 1991 picture of Milt Hinton. "The judge," as musicians admiringly call him, was eighty-one then. He had been a part of much of the history of jazz and was still listening ahead, having recorded with such much younger players as Branford Marsalis. As of this writing, Milt is still enlivening a wide range of combos. I have many photographs of him, but none is as accurate a depiction of the man as Lee's.

Also evocatively accurate is the 1956 shot of Count Basie. Basie was brilliant at knowing what to leave out of his music. He was also laconic off the stand to the point of sometimes appearing to be bland. But he was very astute in the command of his music and musicians, and it is that shrewd intelligence that comes through here. That side of Basie has rarely been captured.

Eric Dolphy's music was always characterized by the "sound of surprise" that is jazz. He discovered sounds—some of them suggested by the sound of birds—that nobody had imagined. And he continually expanded the scope of his instruments so that a Dolphy solo was like a series of discoveries—for himself and his audience. But at the center of what could seem like aggressive dissonance was an extraordinarily gentle, almost innocent, man who bore no malice to anyone. There was an inner serenity that Lee Tanner caught in his 1960 photograph of Eric.

In Art Taylor's book, *Notes and Tunes*, Dizzy Gillespie said, "I go for freedom, but freedom without organization is chaos. [My music] is free, but it's organized freedom."

So, with Lee Tanner's work, there has to be organization in how you see what you want to shoot. But there is also the freedom of spontaneity, knowing when to shoot. Tanner's gift is knowing the moment at which the musician tells his own story—and not only in notes.

—Nat Hentoff

Introduction

This is a book of photographs of my heroes and heroines. These great jazz makers and their music have been a part of my life since I was about seven or eight, when the radio became my constant companion and jazz the music I loved best.

For adventure and mystery I listened to *Jack Armstrong: The All-American Boy, The Shadow,* and *The Green Hornet.* For laughs there were Jack Benny, Edgar Bergen and Charlie McCarthy, and Fred Allen. I also loved baseball: long before I saw a game in Yankee Stadium, I was a devoted Yankees fan because of radio. And there was music: Toscanini conducted the NBC Symphony, and the New York Metropolitan Opera was broadcast every Saturday afternoon. Pop and some swing were to be heard on the *Bob Hope Show* (Stan Kenton was Hope's house bandleader before Les Brown), *The Camel Caravan* with Benny Goodman, and *The Hit Parade,* but for me the revelation came when I discovered jazz. I found the jazz of such greats as Louis Armstrong, Fatha Hines, Sidney Bechet, Basie, Ellington, and Lunceford on a few deejays' shows, on Armed Forces Radio, and on the late-night remote broadcasts from clubs and ballrooms all over the country.

My parents were both born in Russia, thousands of miles apart, and were brought to the United States as infants in the early 1900s. Both families settled in Boston. My father, Vladimir Chenkoff, was an art student at the Boston Museum of Fine Arts in the 1920s and studied with master painter John Singer Sargent, who was in residence doing a series of murals at the Boston Museum, the Boston Public Library, and Harvard University. Vladimir met my mother, Enid Tanner, in the late 1920s. They married in 1930 and moved to New York City.

I was born in May 1931. At about that time my father got his first important commercial assignment, to do advertising illustrations and posters for Charlie Chaplin's film *City Lights.* This led to a series of movie poster commissions over the next ten years that included John Ford's *Stagecoach*, Howard Hawks' *Scarface* (with Paul Muni), and *The Plainsman* (with Gary Cooper). My father also did magazine illustrations. My mother was his agent, and while she was out drumming up new business, I would spend crib-bound hours in the studio, watching my father draw and paint. These were the good times. Unfortunately, my parents had a very stormy marriage, and when things got too difficult my mother would take me back to Boston to stay with her family. We made the round trip more than a few times until finally, in 1937, the split became permanent. My mother and I went to live with my two maiden aunts in the Roxbury section of Boston.

My aunts, Rose and Frieda, were dedicated listeners to classical music: they had plenty of 78s for their marvelous wind-up Victrola and they were season ticket holders for the Boston Symphony. I was surrounded by the music of Bach, Mozart, and Beethoven, and I liked it very much. This appreciation prepared me for the moment when I first tuned into jazz by a chance twist of the radio dial. I sensed that this too was important music, but my aunts didn't share my opinion. So, in the beginning at least, part of why jazz made such an immediate impression on me was because I was rebelling by listening to it. Jazz was something special that I had all to myself. It was my companion.

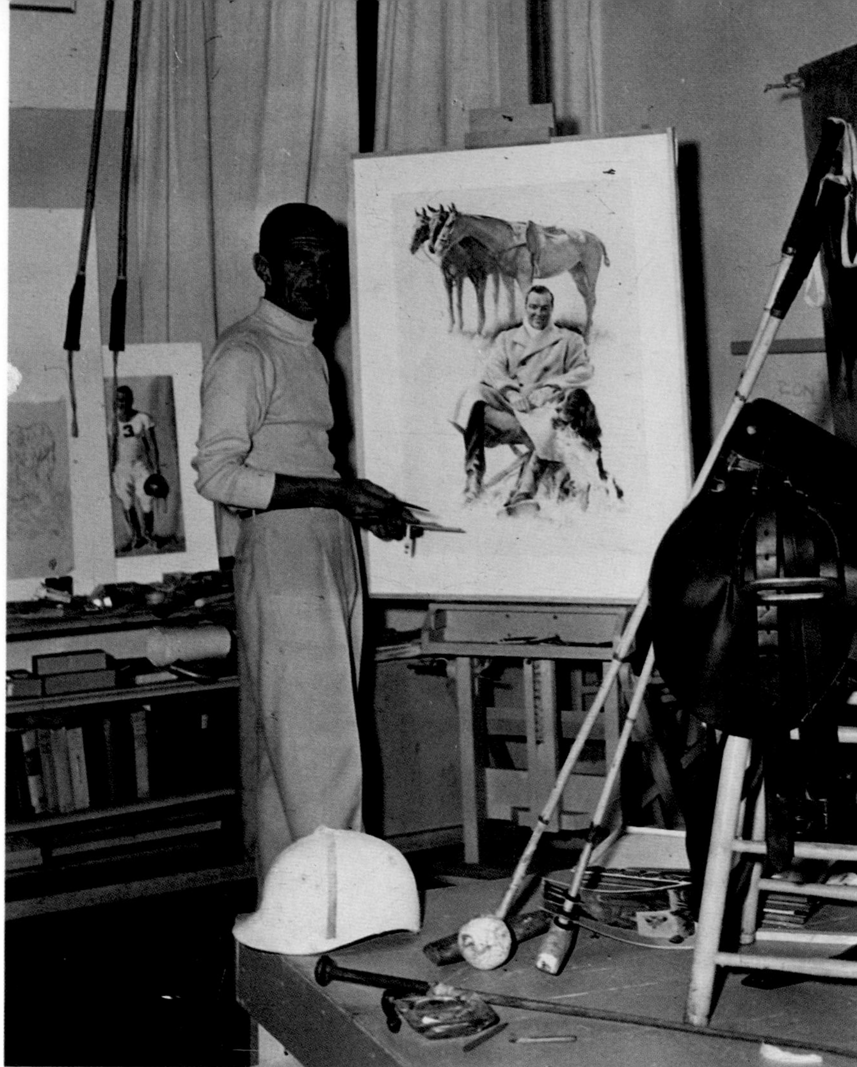

My father in his Delray Beach, Florida, studio in the early 1950s.

Boston has always been a very active jazz town. For example, Bostonians really adored Sidney Bechet. I remember as a youngster, traveling down Massachusetts Avenue on my way to Symphony Hall with my aunts, I saw an enormous banner stretched across the front of the Savoy Cafe at the corner of Columbus Avenue. It announced that Sidney was back in town *again*!...and he'd be in town for months at a time. My exposure to live jazz was at the downtown RKO Boston theater. I would pack a lunch so that I could spend the whole day there, watching show after show with delight and enduring the (usually terrible) movies that played in between. I watched Duke, Count, Benny Goodman, Woody Herman, Cab Calloway, Benny Carter, Cootie Williams, Tommy and Jimmy Dorsey, Gene Krupa, and lots of sweet pop bands like Charlie Spivak and Johnny Long that often had remarkably swinging tunes in their repertoires.

An apprentice milliner in Boston, my mother later got a job at Lord & Taylor, a department store in New York City. We moved back in 1945 and I started high school. My mother firmly steered me toward (in her words) "more substantial educational and career goals," though she didn't discourage my artistic inclinations. I passed the entrance examination for Stuyvesant High School, and while there I began to develop a serious interest in science and math. Years later, I learned that Thelonious Monk had been a Stuyvesant student and so had trombonist Kai Winding. Pianist Richie Powell was my classmate.

Meanwhile, I continued drawing and painting, as well as listening to plenty of jazz. The Fred Robbins *1280 Club* show in the early evening gave me quite an education. With his catholic tastes, Robbins presented the full spectrum of jazz, from old to new. He introduced his radio audience to bebop and gave us an understanding of what we were listening to. It didn't appeal to me at first, but Robbins guided me to full appreciation. If I stayed up late, I would get plenty of bebop from the all-night, all-frantic one, "Symphony Sid" Torin on station WJZ. I also discovered the famous Commodore Record Shop at Forty-second Street and Lexington Avenue, and went there regularly to listen to many recordings in their listening booths. In addition, there were four midtown Manhattan theaters where I went to see and hear the big bands.

A big change in my listening habits came when I learned that the admission requirements were sometimes relaxed at the nightclubs along Fifty-second Street. My buddies and I were just seventeen when we decided to try to spend an evening at the Three Deuces. On that night we were successful: the bartender served us seventy-five-cent Coca-Colas and we listened to a band led by Oscar Pettiford. It wasn't that easy on every excursion, but over the next couple of years I heard Coleman Hawkins, Roy Eldridge, Dizzy Gillespie, Allen Eager, Lucky Thompson, Charlie Parker, and quite a few others. The "Street" went into decline in the late 1940s and strippers replaced the music in one club after another.

The last show that I saw on Fifty-second Street was unforgettable. It was in February 1950 at the Black Orchid, formerly known as the Onyx Club. Pianist Bud Powell's band played magnificently all night to no more than a dozen patrons. The band had Wardell Gray and Sonny Stitt on tenor saxes, Miles Davis on trumpet, Curly Russell on bass, and Roy Haynes on drums. To my delight Powell and Stitt had recorded all the compositions I heard that night for Prestige a month earlier; I still play the disc over and over, remembering that wonderful evening.

By 1948, a new jazz club called the Royal Roost opened on Broadway and it had bleachers where teenagers with limited funds could sit and listen for the price of admission. This was a popular policy that was used later at Birdland. It was not only a boon for the young jazz fans, it gave struggling musicians with limited funds the opportunity to keep up with the music. A regular attraction at the Roost was the great Tadd Dameron band, with Fats Navarro on trumpet and Allen Eager on tenor. Woody Herman brought in his Second Herd, which featured the famous Four Brothers saxophone section. Dizzy's big band played there as well, and it was the place where Miles Davis' Birth of the Cool nonet played its only public performance, for one week.

My interest in photography peaked at this point. Seeing all the remarkable photographs that were published in *Life* and *Look* magazines during the war years, I became intrigued by the dramatic force of candid photography. The ability of photographers like Cartier-Bresson, Ernst Haas, the Capas, Doisneau, Gene Smith, Eve Arnold, Eisenstaedt, Dorothea Lange, Carl Mydans, Roy De Carava, Robert Frank, and others to capture moments of life, from the ordinary to the extraordinary, was remarkable. The few who concentrated on musical subjects gave me further inspiration. In 1944, a "*Life* Goes to a Party" feature was a colossal all-night jam session in photographer Gjon Mili's New York City studio. Everyone seemed to be there, including the relatively unknown Dizzy Gillespie blowing next to Duke at the piano. To me this occasion

Arturo Toscanini, photographed by Robert Hupka. (Courtesy of RCA Victor Records.)

Sidney Bechet, the first jazz musician I heard on the radio when I was seven or eight years old, photographed by Robert Parent.

My first jazz photograph: Bob Brookmeyer on trombone and Wendell Marshall on bass, New York City, in 1953.

marked the birth of jazz photography. Charles Peterson, Bob Parent, Bill Gottlieb, and Herman Leonard were also photographing by the mid-1940s, but like Mili, they were all using big cumbersome cameras and floodlights or flash-guns. With postwar advances in technology that made small cameras with fast lenses affordable and the availability of new fast films, it became possible to shoot using just the ambient light in low-lit club settings. The first available-light pictures of a musician that caught my attention were those by Robert Hupka of Toscanini conducting the NBC Symphony, which were published in *The Saturday Evening Post* in the late 1940s. Later, Bill Claxton's wonderful photos of the West Coast jazz scene began appearing on LP jackets. The culmination of all these changes in photographic styles and aesthetics came in 1955 with Steichen's monumental exhibit "The Family of Man" at New York's Museum of Modern Art. I was already developing my own photographic skills, and seeing this exhibit gave me a powerful push. My all-time favorite picture from that collection (still available in book form) is of an unknown pianist in a dance hall by Ed Feingersh. A close second is Hugh Bell's glorious print of the Tony Scott band, which as I recall was mural-size.

I started with an Argus C3 35mm camera, but then got a Pentacon single-lens reflex 35mm camera with a fast f/2 lens. I took my first jazz pictures in 1953 at an old ballroom in the West Fifties at a bop jam produced by Bob Maltz. Like the weekly traditional jazz jams at the Stuyvesant Casino in lower Manhattan, there was an all-night parade of musicians including Miles Davis, Bob Brookmeyer, Osie Johnson, Wendell Marshall, Horace Silver, and Lou Donaldson. I lost those negatives and only one print (of Brookmeyer, shown at left) remains. Later, fed up with the small 35mm negative size, I switched to a 2¼ × 2¼-inch format using a Mamiya reflex camera. I have stayed with the larger format ever since, and I am happy that I did now that I often make mural-size prints.

From 1949 to 1953 I was a metallurgical engineering student at the old New York University uptown campus in the Bronx, where I deejayed a campus radio show. I worked on the weekends as a salesperson at the Sam Goody record emporium in midtown. The sales staff were classical music students and out-of-work musicians and singers....I was the one-and-only jazz expert. The Manhattan studio musicians would come to me to find the best of the new releases. Goody's would lend me LPs for my radio show in exchange for commercial plugs. There was also a neighborhood jazz clique, and one of the fellows tried to get me started on the tenor sax but I was a poor student.

After graduation I was drafted into the army before I could get my professional career going. Stationed in Virginia with lots of time on my hands, I gave playing music one more chance. I began guitar lessons in D.C. with Sophocles Pappas, who had taught Charlie Byrd. I made better progress this time but as my army tour was ending, I lost interest as I became more concerned with going to graduate school. In 1955, I began materials science studies at the University of Pennsylvania under the GI Bill. The next twenty years would bring marriage, two daughters, a busy career in scientific research in Massachusetts and New Jersey, lots of jazz, photography, and television production.

I returned to Boston in the late 1950s when the jazz scene was bustling. The Connolly brothers gave up the Savoy Cafe, and they opened Connolly's Stardust Room about ten blocks away, at Tremont and Ruggles Streets in Roxbury. Storyville and the Stables in Copley Square also closed, but The Jazz Workshop and Paul's Mall opened on nearby Boylston Street. Meanwhile, north of the city, Lennie Sogoloff made an old roadhouse on Route 1 in Peabody into Lennie's-on-the-Turnpike. Lennie's, the Workshop, and Paul's Mall booked top-flight traveling jazz groups. Connolly's, on the other hand, featured one or two master musicians who played with the house band, which featured pianist/organist Sir Charles Thompson and altoist Jimmy Tyler. The list of visiting legends included Dexter Gordon, Earl Warren, Ben Webster, Coleman Hawkins, Roy Eldridge, Johnny Hodges, Lawrence Brown, Zoot Sims, Booker Ervin, Al Cohn, and many others. Occasionally, when the house band would take a break, there would be superb groups like the Eric Dolphy Quartet, Slide Hampton's Octet, Toshiko Akiyoshi with Charlie Mariano and Sadao Watanabe, Roy Haynes with Frank Strozier, and the Jackie McLean Quartet. A live television show on PBS station WGBH featured one of these local attractions each week. The show, named *Jazz*, was hosted by the Boston University chaplain and ardent jazz fan Fr. Norman O'Connor and, later, by bandleader and teacher Herb Pomeroy. I photographed in all the clubs and in the television studio. By the late 1960s I became the show's producer; the director was David Atwood, well known for his work with *Evening at Pops* and *Nova*. The new program, *Mixed Bag*, was more eclectic. Besides jazz, we featured jazz-rock fusion, blues, and folk music. A short list of guests includes the Charles Lloyd Quartet with Keith Jarrett, avant-gardists

Host Herb Pomeroy (right) interviewing pianist Andrew Hill on *Jazz* at WGBH-TV, Boston, in 1963.

"The Jazz Image" group photo exhibit at Gallery Concord, Concord, California, in August 1991.

Archie Shepp and Roswell Rudd, George Benson jamming with blues legend B.B. King, Jon Hendricks performing his *Evolution of the Blues* suite, Andrew Hill and Bobby Hutcherson, folk singer Livingston Taylor, bluesmen Buddy Guy and Junior Wells, Jeremy Steig's pioneering fusion group Jeremy and the Satyrs, South African pianist Abdullah Ibraham with Joe Farrell and Elvin Jones, and Count's Rock Band, an amazing quartet from within Herbie Mann's band comprised of Larry Coryell on guitar, Steve Marcus on sax, Bobby Moses on drums, and Gene Perla on bass. We also had several remarkable improvisations by a group called Luny Toons. Luny Toons was the brainchild of New England Conservatory academic and Boston Symphony bassist Buell Neidlinger, who had also been a member of avant-garde pianist Cecil Taylor's first group. The ultimate tour-de-force was a production (with special sets and costuming) of Carla Bley's extended piece *A Genuine Tong Funeral* performed by Gary Burton, his quartet, and an ensemble of Berklee College of Music students.

I changed research jobs in 1972, and the family and I moved to New Jersey. Jazz and photography took a back seat as we adjusted to the new location and my new research responsibilities. My daughters went to high school and graduated, but soon divorce split up the family. Daughter Lisa began photographing rock groups in New York City and then went to work for Atlantic Records as a publicist. Younger daughter Dina went to college to study psychology and I moved to Berkeley.

The last sixteen years in California have been the best of my life. Starting over, I soon met my soulmate, Linda, and we married. These days I delight in a busy jazz-related retirement and in the birth of each new grandchild (between us there are eleven). My scientific research accomplishments reached a peak during my last twelve years of full-time work at the University of California's Lawrence Laboratories, and after a brief period of transition, I found I could walk away from what had been a very enjoyable career. What certainly helped was preparing for the retirement by reactivating my interests in jazz and photography. With Linda's encouragement, I began taking pictures again and exhibiting my work. I soon discovered that I enjoyed curating group exhibits. In 1985 I put together a collection of photographs of the late Zoot Sims for a fund raising memorial concert at Kimball's jazz club in San Francisco. What followed was a successful series of group exhibits under the title "The Jazz Image" at the gallery at Kimball's East in Emeryville, the San Francisco Art Commission Gallery, the San Francisco Jazz Festival Gallery, Gallery Concord, the Concord Jazz Festival, the Monterey Jazz Festival, and the Jazz Store Gallery in Carmel. The shows featured the work of Bill Claxton, Herb Snitzer, Herman Leonard, Milt Hinton, Bill Gottlieb, Hugh Bell, Chuck Stewart, Jim Marshall, Carol Friedman, Jerry Stoll, and Kathy Sloane, as well as my own. One exhibit dedicated to Dizzy Gillespie was collected in book form and I expect to do the same for my recent Thelonious Monk show. My ultimate goal is to curate the definitive jazz photography exhibit and to have it travel to the world's museums.

Until that ambition becomes reality, enjoy the pictures of great musicians making jazz that I have gathered to fill the following pages.

—Lee Tanner
Berkeley, California

Photographer Herman Leonard, Dizzy Gillespie, and me at the "Many Views of Dizzy" photo exhibit at Kimball's East, Emeryville, California, in February 1992.

An Ageless Inspiration

Art is speaking from the deepest part of oneself to the deepest part of others.

—source unknown

By 1944, at age thirteen, I had already spent a few years listening to big bands live onstage at the RKO Boston and late at night on the radio, but it would be several more years before I would experience the free-wheeling excitement of live jazz in New York City's nightclubs. Luckily, our radio could pick up shortwave broadcasts and I was able to tune in to *Jubilee*, an armed forces radio program that featured jazz. In 1944 *Jubilee* broadcast the Esquire Jazz Concert from the Metropolitan Opera House in New York City—it was my first jam session and I was blown away. I recently listened to a recording of that concert and it was like unearthing a time capsule. What a treat to reexperience that seminal concert! There they were—Louis "Satchmo" Armstrong, Roy Eldridge, Coleman Hawkins, Jack Teagarden, Lionel Hampton, Red Norvo, Teddy Wilson, Oscar Pettiford, Art Tatum, and Big Sid Catlett—all at the peak of their creativity (which continued for twenty, thirty, and in some cases forty more years, enabling many of us to hear them time and again).

It is an ageless inspiration that drives the great jazz makers. When looking at their lives, you find that they almost invariably began playing professionally in their teens, often needing parental dispensation in order to go on the road with some master musician or well-established band. This magical inspiration stayed with them throughout their lives. It was especially true for Louis Armstrong, who became a beacon for just about everybody—instrumentalists and singers alike—who heard his trumpet and vocal performances and followed in his footsteps. And many did indeed follow.

But jazz is a tough artistic pursuit. The standards are just as high as in any of the arts, with the addition that in jazz you are expected to be brilliant when improvising before a live audience. Writers, poets, painters, and the like at least have the freedom (luxury?) to work and rework their creations in private. (In music, of course, the parallel is studio recording sessions.) Furthermore, jazz is a relatively small subset of music that is still linked with the commercial entertainment world and all its pressures. Hence, success is too often measured by unit sales and audience numbers, and not by strictly aesthetic values. Moreover, since jazz is largely an outgrowth of African-American culture in the United States, black jazz players still suffer the effects of a pervasive racism. However, when drummer Papa Jo Jones reflected on the jazz life, he said, "For all the pain and problems we endured being black men in America, we really had some wonderful times." That's because jazz making is a joyful, transcendent artistic pursuit.

The transition that took place from the thirties to the forties, when I first heard jazz, was provocative. Changes in the music were in the air, though it took me a while to catch on. Listening to the 1944 Esquire concert now, I readily hear the new phrases of the burgeoning bebop style, particularly in compositions by tenor saxophonist Coleman Hawkins and bassist Oscar Pettiford. Hawkins (known as "The Bean" because of his intelligence) was Pettiford's senior by twenty years, but he was very much in sync with the innovations of the time. He had just returned from an extended hiatus in Europe and jumped into the New York jazz scene with both feet. He collaborated with such young lions as trumpeter Dizzy Gillespie, saxophonist Don Byas, pianist Thelonious Monk, and drummer Max Roach. As time went on, Hawkins always put himself into new and challenging situations, for example teaming up with John Coltrane to work with Monk on some difficult music. Later, he worked with Max Roach on Max's ambitious and controversial *Freedom Now Suite*, giving the section entitled "Driva Man" a power of expression no one else could have given it. Throughout his life he remained a vital, commanding, inspirational, and majestic figure.

From the 1940s on Hawkins had a compatriot, a collaborator made in heaven, a perfect foil in the trumpet giant Roy "Little Jazz" Eldridge. Jazz impresario Norman Granz said that Roy most typifies jazz: "He's a musician for whom it's far more important to dare. To try to reach a particular peak...even if he falls on his ass in the attempt...than it is to play safe." This, by definition, is the ageless inspiration. When I first heard him with the Gene Krupa band, I was astonished by the sheer exuberance of his playing. I heard the same spirited playing when he teamed with Hawkins, Johnny Hodges, Zoot Sims, Stan Getz, and Count Basie. Nat Hentoff recalled that during a fifties TV rehearsal Roy played with every bit of his astonishing energy. Roy said, "I can never say all I want to say." Nat's observation: "So he kept on trying to." It is easy to see why Dizzy Gillespie (among many others) was so enthralled by Roy.

In the early thirties, Henry "Red" Allen was another excellent Hawkins collaborator, but the team broke up when Hawkins left for Europe. A proud, gentle,

OPPOSITE: Coleman Hawkins, Connolly's, Boston, 1958

and shy man offstage, Red was flamboyant in the spotlight. A dedicated showman like his idol Armstrong, Allen built a successful career with performances in New York City in the clubs on Fifty-second Street and at the Metropole, often backed by trombonist J.C. Higginbotham. Red was appreciated by modernists. He had great confidence in his ability and was serious about his playing. Dizzy recalls, "A few of the older guys started playing our riffs, like Henry 'Red' Allen." Miles Davis listened intently, as did avant-garde trumpeter Don Ellis, who felt that in the fifties Allen was the most creative player in New York. Indeed, with perhaps only ten more years to play, Red was experiencing a renaissance. Delightfully, he and Coleman Hawkins got together again in 1957 and, along with Higginbotham and drummer Cozy Cole, outdid themselves on a series of RCA recordings.

Charlie Shavers, a technically fluid and energetic trumpeter, was another important voice in the thirties/forties transition. A mainstay of the popular John Kirby "Biggest Little Band" from 1937 to 1944, Shavers then became the featured soloist in the Tommy Dorsey band. He also found time to record in excellent pick-up sessions (for instance on the bop anthem "Salt Peanuts," with the Auld-Hawkins-Webster Saxtet). The most exciting display of both his ability to jam and to play ballads is found on the takes (and outtakes) of a 1945 session with Nat "King" Cole on piano, Herbie Haymer on tenor sax, John Simmons on bass, and an explosive, driving Buddy Rich on drums. Everyone was on for this one afternoon of recording (it's probably the best recorded example of King Cole's playing).

I cannot forget Sidney Bechet, who was the first instrumentalist I really took notice of when I started listening to jazz. The record programs on Boston radio seemed to feature him even more than Louis Armstrong. Unfortunately, as was the case with Armstrong and Lester Young, I did not get the chance to photograph him. His wonderfully emotional playing of the soprano sax still thrills me. One of my all-time favorite jazz performances is his gorgeously sultry version of Gershwin's "Summertime." I don't think anyone has been able to match Bechet on what is widely considered a difficult instrument to master, although John Coltrane, Zoot Sims, Steve Lacy, and Woody Herman were all successful in finding their own way of expressing themselves on the soprano.

Earl "Fatha" Hines was profoundly influenced by Louis Armstrong's rhythmic and harmonic discoveries, and was himself a brilliant prime mover in the development of jazz piano. Hines worked with Louis in the twenties and it was one of the great musical pairings. Hines constantly challenged Satchmo to stretch himself, and they astounded everyone with the possibilities of jazz soloing. In the late forties they teamed up again: Hines joined trombonist Jack Teagarden and clarinetist Barney Bigard in the Armstrong All Stars Band. In between, starting in 1929, Hines led a fine big band. "It was a very hot band," said Hines. "That's why the people were all so happy in those days. Nobody slept at the Grand Terrace [in Chicago]." From the thirties to the early forties the band was an incubator for the jazz-to-come, bebop. Saxophonist Budd Johnson was the musical director; on trumpet were Dizzy Gillespie and Benny Harris; Charlie "Bird" Parker played tenor sax; and Billy Eckstine and Sarah Vaughn sang. The musically ambitious Eckstine, who also played trombone and trumpet, spun the youngsters off into a band of his own in the mid-forties. It was the first band dedicated to bebop.

Still creative in the sixties but fed up with the lack of good playing opportunities, Hines was ready to quit music. Just in time, however, writer and friend Stanley Dance set up two concerts at New York City's Little Theater and once again an appreciative audience heard Fatha's genius. Doug Ramsey wrote, "Even Armstrong stopped developing long before he reached his seventies. But Hines at seventy-four shows no sign of diminishing powers....He can scare the hell out of you with his creativity." He died at age eighty.

Then there's bassist Milt Hinton, now in his mid-eighties and still very much on the scene. Milt was a boyhood friend of Benny Goodman in Chicago and a buddy of Dizzy Gillespie when they were in Cab Calloway's band in the early forties. Dizzy, as was his way, would share his new ideas, encourage Milt to use them, and help him with his playing style. Milt was tired of traveling, so he settled in New York City in the fifties and became the number one bass player on call for jobs. He backed just about everyone, from pop singers Bobby Darin and Barbra Streisand to blues diva Dinah Washington to mainstreamers Pee Wee Russell, Max Kaminsky, and Coleman Hawkins to avant-garde modernists George Russell and the Sandole Brothers. Very much a labor and civil rights activist, Milt worked to break the color line in the radio and television industry. And all during these years, since the late thirties, he has photographed the jazz scene from his unique vantage point as a musician. His two books, *Bass Line* and *Over Time*, are joy-filled pictorials of the family of jazz. He is still playing, photographing, and teaching, often working with younger musicians such as Branford Marsalis.

Pee Wee Russell was a mainstay of the Eddie Condon Chicago Dixieland gang, but late in life, Russell branched out with trombonist Marshall Brown to play modern compositions by Coltrane, Ornette Coleman, and others. He also performed wonderfully with Monk at the 1963 Newport Jazz Festival. Saxophonist Bud Freeman said, "Pee Wee, with all his nervous playing and without any facility, had more to say than any of the technicians."

Almost ninety, Benny Carter is still active and is a remarkable soloist on alto sax and trumpet. Over his seven-plus decade career he has written and arranged hundreds of songs for big bands, small combos, and singers, as well as writing several film scores. He is a true man for all seasons and a personification of the ageless inspiration in jazz.

The product of the marvelously experimental thirties and forties period was bebop. An academic description of this jazz style was offered by Gary Giddins: "Bebop, a music that had the effect of dissecting the jazz of the swing era and putting it together in a new way. Harmonically it took the largest and ineluctable leap from a diatonic riff-based music of few chords and fewer keys to a labyrinthine chromaticism with elaborate chord substitutions and a marked preference for the diminished scale....A new virtuosity was required to play them...and Dizzy Gillespie and Charlie Parker brought fresh fevers to jazz with their stunning articulation and range." While accurate, it is perhaps not all that easy to comprehend. Dizzy said, "It's hard to say in words how our music came together. When I found out how Charlie Parker played, it was just what I needed to put with my contribution." Like Coleman Hawkins and Thelonious Monk, Dizzy was a teacher. My choice for the definitive musical example of the period would be a 1945 recording session entitled *Red Norvo's Fabulous Jam Session*. It teamed Bird and Dizzy with "traditionalist" Norvo on vibes.

Earl
Hines,
WBZ-TV,
Boston,
1963

Milt Hinton,
Kimball's East,
Emeryville,
California, 1991

No music is my music.
It's everybody's who
can feel it. You're
here...well if there's
music, you feel it—
then it's yours, too.

—Sidney Bechet, soprano saxophonist, clarinetist

Roy Eldridge, Connolly's, Boston, 1958

Charlie Shavers, Tony Eire, and Alan Dawson, WGBH-TV, Boston, 1967

OPPOSITE: Henry "Red" Allen, Connolly's, Boston, 1958

Benny Carter, Kimball's East,
Emeryville, California, 1994

You've got to love to be able to play.

—Louis Armstrong,
trumpeter, singer

Budd Johnson, Connolly's, Boston, 1966

Pee Wee Russell,
Lennie's-on-the-Turnpike,
West Peabody,
Massachusetts, 1965

Duke Ellington

After hearing what Ellington can do with fourteen players, the average modern composer who splashes about with eighty players in the Respighi manner must feel a little chastened.

—Constant Lambert, composer

Nat Hentoff said, "Ellington was a man who was an orchestra." Duke was the most gifted composer in jazz, and his orchestra—not the piano—was his primary instrument. He staffed it with virtuosos: wonderful musicians for whom he could tailor music, and who collectively provided him with the ultimate in instantaneous musical feedback. Over the years, many musicians came to play for Duke, and most stayed for the duration. As Barney Bigard said, "I started that Friday and ended fourteen years later." Others who went the distance with the Duke included trombonist Lawrence Brown and reed players Harry Carney, Jimmy Hamilton, Russell Procope, and Johnny Hodges. To me alto saxophonist Hodges was the quintessential Ellingtonian. In his early years, he was a student of Sidney Bechet and this experience was always evident in Hodges' poignant lyricism and his mastery of the blues. If tenor saxist Lester Young was a dancer, a Nijinsky, then Hodges was an operatic diva, a Lily Pons.

Tenor saxophonist Ben Webster left the band after only a few years' stay in the late thirties to forties, but he has always been identified as an Ellingtonian. Who can think of the recordings of the compositions "Cottontail," "Chelsea Bridge," "Conga Brava," "Raincheck," and many others from that period without recalling Webster? Al Sears took Ben's chair in 1943; Ben returned briefly in 1948; and the spot was later filled by Paul Gonsalves in 1953. Paul stayed, and he soon became a crowd-pleasing workhorse known for his wild and woolly solo in the wailing interval of Duke's "Crescendo and Diminuendo in Blue." Ray Nance provided superb trumpet and violin statements for Ellington's compositions as well as humorous breaks with his occasional singing and dancing. Two other master trumpeters also filled out the Duke's traveling composer's workshop: Cootie Williams and Clark Terry. Williams, who replaced growl-mute expert Bubber Miley in 1929, spent a remarkable eleven years with the Duke before joining Benny Goodman's band. Williams sparked Goodman's sextet working with guitar pioneer Charlie Christian and tenor saxist Georgie Auld. Cootie then led an excellent band of his own for many years; he was also the first to record Thelonious Monk's music. He rejoined the Ellington band in 1962 and remained till his death in the late seventies. Clark Terry's tenure was shorter, but his unique voice was an integral part of Ellington's longer pieces of the 1950s such as "Such Sweet Thunder" and "A Drum Is a Woman."

The music that Duke and his alter ego Billy Strayhorn created, and that the band played, was marvelous. My favorites are usually a matter of what I am listening to at the moment. Furthermore, I adore the way Ellington played piano. The stride-style roots were there along with his romantic harmonic approach, and the melody was always within reach. Despite his reluctance to be considered as such, there is simply no doubt that Duke Ellington was a major pianist. If you need any proof of this, just listen to his duos with bassist Jimmy Blanton and later with Ray Brown, the trio recording with Charles Mingus and Max Roach, his pairings with Coleman Hawkins and John Coltrane, and the most recently discovered gem of a solo performance at New York City's Whitney Museum in 1972, two years before his death.

OPPOSITE: Duke Ellington, Newport Jazz Festival, Newport, Rhode Island, 1962

Buescher

Johnny Hodges,
Connolly's,
Boston, 1961

He [Hodges] says what he wants to say on his horn, and that is it. He says it in his language, which is specific, and you could say that he is pure artistry.

—Duke Ellington,
composer, bandleader, pianist

Cootie Williams,
Connolly's,
Boston, 1959

When Duke would be playing he'd [Nance] do a kind of jig, peckin' round the stage, and every time he'd shoot his cuffs he made his coat tail go up. Then he'd pull his coat down—and up went his cuffs! I used to go into hysterics every night.

—Jack Fallon, bassist

Ray Nance,
The Fenway Theater,
Boston, 1958

Ben Webster,
Connolly's,
Boston, 1962

Duke Ellington,
The Fenway Theater,
Boston, 1958

OPPOSITE: The Ellington Band with guest soloist Gerry Mulligan, Boston Globe Jazz Festival, Boston, 1967

I'm a piano player, a rehearsal piano player, a jive-time conductor, bandleader, and sometimes I just do nothing but take bows...and I have fun. My, my, my. My thing is having fun.

—Duke Ellington, composer, bandleader, pianist

Count Basie, The Bluenote, Chicago, 1956

Count Basie

One night in 1939 at the Famous Door on Fifty-second Street...The [Basie] sound was so great, so intense, that it became almost solid enough to walk through. Out of this acoustical wave Prez...rose and whispered, "How do you do there!" It cut through the brass like a bullet, soft as it was, and hit me in the pit of the stomach....I almost cried.

—Ralph Gleason, writer

Unlike Ellington's band, which featured Duke's subtle and complex music, the Basie band focused on a simplicity of structure, format, and texture. It was a veritable swing machine fueled by blues-based arrangements made by committee. These arrangements (called "head" arrangements) were constructed section by section from the best of a soloist's riffs rather than written out by a single arranger's hand. Hentoff, paraphrasing trombonist Dickie Wells, said, "In all those hours of playing and jamming, countless phrases were offered, modified, rejected and perfected. The good ones were remembered and formed a common language." The driving engine of the machine was an amazing rhythm section that rode along on a smooth 4/4 beat that was remarkably consistent and even. Musician Gene Ramey said that Basie bassist Walter Page organized them, made them think of restraint, and kept drummer Jo Jones—who was full of pep—in tow. Page made sure you could hear each rhythm-section instrument, and then Basie—with his spare piano interjections—gave the piece its direction. This team, combined with what Hentoff has called "a floating, subtly unpredictable band of instrumental dancers," provided the arena for the remarkable solos from Harry Edison, Buck Clayton, Earl Warren, Herschel Evans, Buddy Tate, and—most amazing of all—tenor saxophonist and clarinetist Lester Young. Doug Ramsey once called Young "a ballet dancer who leaped and swooped with such grace across the bar lines," and observed that "Young glided through his solo statements."

Commenting on how the Basie band changed over time, Gunther Schuller said, "The old band played with more spirit, more individuality, more spontaneity...a small, loose big band filled with soloists. The blary roughness of the thirties/forties band gave way [in the fifties and beyond] to a polished more balanced sound...powerful, rich, full-bodied...with technically more accomplished players." To my mind, the subsequent generation of soloists—including Eddie "Lockjaw" Davis, Thad Jones, Frank Foster, and Al Grey—were certainly excellent, though somehow not as spellbinding as the instrumental voices of the earlier era. Basie made sure the band rarely played over the audience's head. He retained a solid staff of arrangers to provide a dependable rhythmic and melodic style that was very attractive and contagious—and always, always swinging. As George Simon commented, "Few leaders in [jazz] history ever walked the tightrope between commercial appeal and musical integrity as daintily and yet as assuredly as Count Basie." Even now, without the leadership of "The Chief" (as he was lovingly known), the band keeps its fans happily satisfied.

Another essential ingredient of the band's performances during most of its years was provided by the superb singers; early on it was Helen Humes and "Little" Jimmy Rushing. Rushing, who started out as a ballad singer, sang the blues with a certain panache, a special touch of elegance. Then in the fifties there was the magnificent Joe Williams. Leslie Gourse commented that the blues hits of the Basie/Williams team had a loud swing that made your heart beat faster and your skin tingle. She also wrote about Williams singing (a cappella) "Come Sunday," which was Duke Ellington's prayer for his people: "It proved he has the most gorgeous voice, dramatic presence and lovable sensibility of any man in entertaining outside of opera."

Basie, like Ellington, often soft-pedaled his piano playing, but in later years he made several truly memorable recordings, paired with Oscar Peterson, as a soloist with rhythm section and also accompanying such superb instrumentalists as Zoot Sims, Lockjaw Davis, and Joe Pass.

Buck Clayton, Connolly's, Boston, 1957

Buddy Tate, WGBH-TV, Boston, 1966

Harry "Sweets" Edison, Connolly's, Boston, 1958

Basie never told you to play with a mute, or to play open, all he'd tell you was take four or five choruses. All he wanted you to do was swing.

—"Sweets" Edison, trumpeter

Jimmy Rushing and Budd Johnson,
WGBH-TV, Boston, 1966

Joe Williams,
WGBH-TV,
Boston, 1968

Joe Williams sings with peerless grace and feeling....[He] grabs the heart of a song with simple eloquence. He makes every phrase matter. No wasted motion.

—Jesse Hamlin, writer

The Basie Band, Boston Globe Jazz Festival, Boston, 1967

Woody Herman, Paramus High School, Paramus, New Jersey, 1977

Woody Herman

Have you caught that Herman Herd yet? WOWIE!!

—Overheard on Fifty-second Street in 1945

In 1942 I saw Woody's Band That Plays The Blues at the RKO Boston. I recall it was quite good, but didn't turn me around as the Basie or Ellington bands did. Then in the summer of 1944, a friend of mine came back from vacation in Virginia, and just could not stop raving about the current Herman band. My friend, a drum freak, was first treated to a night of the Tommy Dorsey band with Buddy Rich at a dance pavilion, and thought he was in heaven. The next night, however, Woody roared in with drummer Davey Tough driving a brand new collection of exciting young musicians. "Wild men!" my friend called them. That fall I moved to New York City and got my first taste of the Herman Herd when they performed at the Paramount Theater. The intoxicating enthusiasm they exhibited is still beyond description. To this day I have not heard a trumpet section quite like that one! The bop influence of Dizzy was profound. And Sonny Berman's trumpet solos were remarkable.

Sonny Berman's powerhouse playing on "Ah Your Father's Moustache" was filled with humor, and his savage intensity on "Sidewalks of Cuba" just tore through the ensembles. Expressing his softer side, Sonny's ballads were gentle, emotional—almost tearful—outpourings: listen to him on guitarist Billy Bauer's "Pam," on two gorgeous pieces by Ralph Burns, "Nocturne" and "Introspection." Sonny's playing always reminded me of a Yiddish *schrai*...a Jewish cry. Ira Gitler confirmed this view: "The intervals and inflections [of Sonny's playing] have moved more than one observer to draw analogies with Jewish liturgical music and the patterns and timbre of a fine cantor." Unfortunately, his full potential was never to be realized: Berman died at twenty-two, leaving only a few memorable recordings. The other showstopping soloists were Flip Phillips on tenor sax, Bill Harris on trombone, Red Norvo on vibes, and Pete Condoli on trumpet.

In a sense, the band had a Basie-type flow and swing, and like Basie's crew, the Herd made the most of the spontaneity of head arrangements. Woody said, "Ideas and whole new tunes sprang out of that group like sparks. Flip would blow something, Pete or Neal [Hefti] would grab it, and the first you knew we had a new number." There were overtones of Ellington as well, particularly on ballads where Woody's alto sax playing was a loving tribute to Johnny Hodges. There was no mistaking, however, that the Herd had an overwhelming musical identity and energy all its own. Woody took a break in 1946, but he was back in 1948 with a second monster group, mostly youngsters who were more influenced by bebop than their predecessors had been. This band was facilitating the transition from swing to bop, but it was not a dedicated bebop big band in the same sense that the groups led by Gillespie and Billy Eckstine were. The Herd's trademark powerhouse trumpets were back, now joined by a unique saxophone section of Lester Young and Charlie Parker offsprings: Herbie Steward, Stan Getz, and Zoot Sims (and, later, Al Cohn) on tenors and Serge Chaloff on baritone. These men were known as The Four Brothers. Bill Harris, bassist Chubby Jackson, drummer Don Lamond, and trumpeter Shorty Rogers returned. New players were vibraphonist Terry Gibbs and trumpeter Red Rodney. Later there were Gene Ammons, Shelly Manne, Milt Jackson, and Oscar Pettiford. Zoot summed up the experience so well: "I loved that band! We were all young and had the same ideas. I'd always worried about what other guys were thinking in all the bands I'd been in, and in Woody's I found out: they were thinking the same thing I was."

The first and second editions of the Herman Herd were the beginning of thirty years of Woody's traveling musical academies. Young players would join, learn the discipline, find their identities, and then move on to experience their own greatness. In this regard, the Herman Herds were very much like Art Blakey's Jazz Messengers, and Woody was the ideal "road father," a mentor who got enormous satisfaction out of seeing his kids blossom. As an example, just listen to the Third Herd members rise to the occasion on a one-night stand in Kansas City with Charlie Parker as soloist (on a 1996 release on Drive Archive Records).

Each evolution of the band—up to and including the most recent Young Thundering Herd (still playing after Woody's death)—has been superb. However, in my view, the 1950s aggregations with many of Boston's Berklee School of Music faculty members and former students (Phil Wilson on trombone; Bill Chase and Dusko Goykevich on trumpet; Sal Nistico, Jimmy Mosher, and Andy McGee on sax; and Jake Hanna on drums) rank a close second with the best of the First and Second Herds. I guess this isn't surprising, since the first two were the bands that I grew up with. I was coming of age as they were. Jazz is such a passionate art, and I'll always remember those performances as I will my first taste of love.

Don
Lamond,
WGBH-TV,
Boston,
1966

Terry Gibbs, The Jazz Workshop, Boston, 1965

Dusko Goykovich and John Neves, Connolly's, Boston, 1962

All over the world people talk about my Dream Band and I appreciate it. But that Second Herd was one of the greatest bands of all time. Besides the many great soloists, it was one of the greatest *ensemble* bands! And that was because of Woody Herman.

—Terry Gibbs, vibraphonist, bandleader

Stan Getz,
Newport Jazz Festival,
Newport, 1964

Al Cohn, Connolly's, Boston, 1963

Zoot Sims,
Connolly's,
Boston, 1961

I went with Woody and became one of the Four Brothers [sax section]. I loved that band! We were all young and had the same ideas. I'd always worried about what other guys were thinking in all the bands I'd been in, and in Woody's I found out: they were thinking the same thing I was.

—Zoot Sims, saxophonist

Gene Ammons,
Connolly's,
Boston, 1958

Sal Nistico, The Wagon Wheels, Peabody, Massachusetts, 1963

Bill Perkins and Conte Candoli,
Palo Alto Community Center, Palo Alto, California, 1995

Nobody does what Woody does as well as he does. If we could only figure out what it is that he does.

—Phil Wilson, trombonist, arranger, teacher

Dizzy Gillespie

A great figure in American music, in world music, perhaps the greatest innovator of recent times.

—Martin Williams, writer

In the forties Dizzy Gillespie seemed to be everywhere, bouncing from one big band to another trying to inject his new musical ideas into everyone's consciousness and getting his arrangements into their repertoires. He played with, sat in with, and/or arranged for the bands of Les Hite, Teddy Hill, Lucky Millinder, Cab Calloway, Duke Ellington, Charlie Barnet, Earl Hines, Billy Eckstine, Boyd Raeburn, Georgie Auld, Oscar Pettiford, and Woody Herman. When with Calloway, Gillespie became an eager student of Afro-Cuban music with Cuban trumpet master and bandmate Mario Bauza as his teacher. Latin stylings became a major thrust of his music for the rest of his life and a major part of the repertoire of his first big band, which lasted from 1945 to 1949.

Throughout the forties, Dizzy was also working and recording with small bands on Fifty-second Street and, of course, jamming uptown at Minton's. Finally, he connected with Charlie "Bird" Parker and they worked their magic as a team for several years. While Dizzy was the proactive teacher, Bird's influence was by example. Parker just played and people listened—and they heard. Even before he was known by name, musicians discovered him on late-night radio and were astonished by what amazing things this new cat with Jay McShann's band was doing on alto sax. Ralph Gleason commented, "The only thing consistent about Charlie Parker was his music....He lived in the music in a way he never ever did as a person."

Dizzy's forties big band was a great crowd pleaser, sometimes a little ragged, but driven and wildly enthusiastic. Over a period of four years it was staffed by a *Who's Who* of the new music: Thelonious Monk and John Lewis on piano; Milt Jackson on vibes; Ray Brown, Al McKibbon, and Percy Heath on bass; Kenny Clarke, Joe Harris, and Teddy Stewart on drums; James Moody, Cecil Payne, "Big Nick" Nicholas, Ernie Henry, Jimmy Heath, Paul Gonsalves, Budd Johnson, and John Coltrane on sax; Dave Burns, Elmon Wright, Willie Cook, Benny Harris, and Benny Bailey on trumpet; J.J. Johnson, Taswell Baird, and Matthew Gee on trombone; and of course the powerful rhythms of Chano Pozo on congas. I enjoyed them all immensely, but at the time my heart and soul belonged to Woody Herman's First and Second Herds. It was only much later that I could fully appreciate what treats I had been lucky to experience; fortunately many were recorded and I could revisit them. Dizzy put another big band on the road in the mid-fifties, and traveled internationally under the auspices of the State Department. This time he had trumpeters Lee Morgan, Joe Gordon, and Quincy Jones; trombonist Melba Liston, who also arranged the band's music (as did Quincy Jones and Ernie Wilkins); saxists Benny Golson, Billy Mitchell, and Phil Woods; pianist Wynton Kelly; and drummer Charlie Persip.

By the 1950s, after his association with Chano Pozo, Gillespie became the quasi-official godfather of Latin music. Arranger/composer Chico O'Farrell wrote the *Afro-Cuban Suite* for Dizzy, and the recordings of the suite featured Gillespie's mentor Mario Bauza and the trumpeter's latest Cuban discovery, congero Candido Camero. Later, in the 1960s, Argentine pianist Lalo Schifrin composed *The Gillespiana Suite* and *The New Continent*. Lalo became a member of the quintet that is my favorite of all the combos Dizzy put together. It had very strong, individualistic players: either Leo Wright or James Moody on alto sax, Chris White on bass, and Rudy Collins on drums (later, Kenny Barron replaced Schifrin). Like Stan Getz and Charlie Byrd, Dizzy had discovered Brazilian music and he interpreted it beautifully. The live recordings from New York's Museum of Modern Art and from a festival on the French Riviera feature absolutely wonderful performances by all involved.

For the next three decades, Dizzy continued to be the ubiquitous master performer and teacher. He participated in lots of loose jamming sessions with Norman Granz's in-house staff of superstars, including Sonny Rollins, Sonny Stitt, Benny Carter, Oscar Peterson, and Joe Pass. Gillespie made recordings with Machito, performed another suite by Lalo Schifrin, and partook in many wonderful tours in Europe in the 1980s and 1990s. In the last years of his life he fronted the United Nation Orchestra, which was under the musical direction of alto saxophonist Paquito D'Rivera and trombonist Slide Hampton. Today, the spirits of both Dizzy and Bird are still on the road, in the music played by Hampton's new star-studded JazzMasters ensemble.

OPPOSITE: Dizzy Gillespie, The Jazz Workshop, Boston, 1963

OPPOSITE: Melba Liston, Connolly's, Boston, 1962

Junior Mance, WGBH-TV, Boston, 1967

The three years I spent with Dizzy were more valuable than all the years I spent in any other musical instruction.

—Junior Mance, pianist

James Moody and Bill Bell, Herbst Theater, San Francisco, 1990

Every time I get on the bandstand with him [Dizzy] is a musical lesson. Sometimes little bits of wisdom he imparts will come back to me years later and I'll say, "Ah!"

—James Moody, saxophonist

Sonny Stitt, Newport Jazz Festival, Newport, 1962

I've always been a Latin [music] freak. I realized that our music and that of our Latin American brothers had a common source. The Latin musician was fortunate in one sense. They didn't take the drum away from him, so he was polyrhythmic.

—Dizzy Gillespie, trumpeter, composer, bandleader

OPPOSITE: Candido Camero, Connolly's, Boston, 1961

Stitt...was the first, and is still the best, of Charlie Parker's countless followers...

—Whitney Balliett, writer

LEFT TO RIGHT: James Moody, Kenny Barron, Dizzy Gillespie, Rudy Collins, and Chris White, Lennie's-on-the-Turnpike, West Peabody, Massachusetts, 1963

51

Cecil
Payne,
Connolly's,
Boston,
1958

Dizzy Gillespie,
WGBH-TV,
Boston, 1964

[Dizzy] had the vocation to teach and he went about unraveling bop's often convoluted harmonies as if the future of jazz depended on his ability to make first and second generation boppers understand what they were doing.

—Doug Ramsey, writer

Dizzy Gillespie, Newport Jazz Festival,
Newport, 1963

Thelonious Monk

I say play your own way. Don't play what the public wants...you play what you want and let the public pick up on what you are doing, even if it does take them fifteen, twenty years.

—Thelonious Monk, pianist, composer

OPPOSITE: Thelonious Monk, WGBH-TV, Boston, 1968

Monk's playing and his music were the most unusual that I had ever heard in or out of jazz. Martin Williams said, "Monk's style, like Lester Young's in the late thirties, depends on surprise." That certainly was part of the reason I liked his piano playing and compositions immensely from the start. The visceral feelings stimulated by the music grabbed you and insisted that you pay attention. Clearly, Thelonious Monk was an original, an innovative force comparable in many ways to Duke Ellington. Monk taught his musicians and encouraged them to develop and to excel, but when they played *with* him, they were constrained to play in the manner that he wanted. This wasn't always easy. Johnny Griffin, a former band member said, "You can play Monk's music with other musicians and it's fantastic...'cause it's completely different. But playing with him at the piano...I found it difficult at times, I mean DIFFICULT!....With him comping it can be quite overwhelming." Griffin also said, "It was one of the greatest experiences of my life to play with Thelonious. Not only that he is my favorite musician...it was his personality, his humor."

Perhaps the clearest example of Monk's strength was in the wonderful recordings he made with saxophonist Gerry Mulligan, a man of very strong personality himself. Gerry is definitely in Thelonious' hip pocket throughout the recordings. Monk often did the same with Coltrane and Rollins (and even with Coleman Hawkins and traditional clarinetist Pee Wee Russell). However, when it was time for the players to leave his group, Monk sent them out with a vivid sense of themselves; the subsequent accomplishments of Coltrane and Rollins bear this out. In 1961, Monk was joined by saxist Charlie Rouse in a blessed collaboration that lasted into Monk's last years of playing. It was as if Rouse owned the road map to Monk's imagination; listen to any of the recordings with Rouse and you will recognize this empathy.

Monk's musical accomplishments were remarkable. Besides his own compositions, he interpreted his idol Ellington's music on piano with loving care. He also had a way of reworking old (in some cases, really old) standard melodies with breathtaking originality and humor. After his treatment, tunes like "Tea for Two," "Sweet and Lovely," "Don't Blame Me," and "Memories of You" became his property. The instrumental influences on Monk go back to the great stride pianists James P. Johnson, Willie "The Lion" Smith, bluesman Jimmy Yancy, and of course Ellington. However, with Monk's unique spin, as Joe Goldberg said, "The result is a jagged, humorous, powerfully swinging music that always sounds like a wryly amused commentary on itself."

Singer and pianist Carmen McRae said, "His music made me smile." The Goldberg description fits the group performances on the "Brilliant Corners" recording sessions. Trumpeter Clark Terry, with his Ellington background, fits in so well on the exotic composition "Bemsha Swing." Later, Terry uses Monk's pianistics as a wonderful interactive foil for his fluegelhorn playing on his own recording entitled "In Orbit."

Monk's influence on other pianists was quite profound, as can be heard in the work of Randy Weston, Mal Waldron, Horace Silver, Cecil Taylor, Jessica Williams, and Andrew Hill. Monk said, "When I was a kid, I felt something had to be done about all that jazz. So I've been doing it for twenty years. Maybe I've turned jazz another way. Maybe I'm a major influence. I don't know. Anyway, my music is my music. Jazz is my adventure. I'm after new chords, new ways of syncopating, new figurations, new runs. How to use notes differently. That's it. Just how to use notes differently."

Johnny Griffin, Connolly's, Boston, 1958

> You can play Monk's music with other musicians and it's fantastic...'cause it's completely different. But playing with him at the piano...I found it difficult at times, I mean DIFFICULT!....With him comping it can be quite overwhelming.
>
> —**Johnny Griffin, saxophonist**

Clark Terry, Connolly's, Boston, 1960

Charlie Rouse,
WGBH-TV,
Boston, 1968

Andrew Hill and Cecil McBee, WGBH-TV, Boston, 1967

I could go by Monk's house and all the guys would be there. We would sit and listen to him play. We had a tribal thing going. It wasn't planned like that, but it was something that happened. It was our culture. I look upon this music [jazz] as our [Afro-American] folk music.

—Randy Weston, pianist, composer

OPPOSITE: Randy Weston and Ernie Shepard, WGBH-TV, Boston, 1967

Thelonious Monk, WGBH-TV, Boston, 1968

[I asked Monk] were you ever taught to hold your hands in the formal manner [when playing]? He then asked me, "That's how you're supposed to ?" feigning wide-eyed surprise. "I hold them any way I feel like holding 'em. I hit the piano with my elbow sometimes because of a certain sound I want to hear, certain chords. You can't hit that many notes with your hands. Sometimes people laugh when I'm doing that. Yeah, let 'em laugh! They need something to laugh at."

—Valerie Wilmer, writer

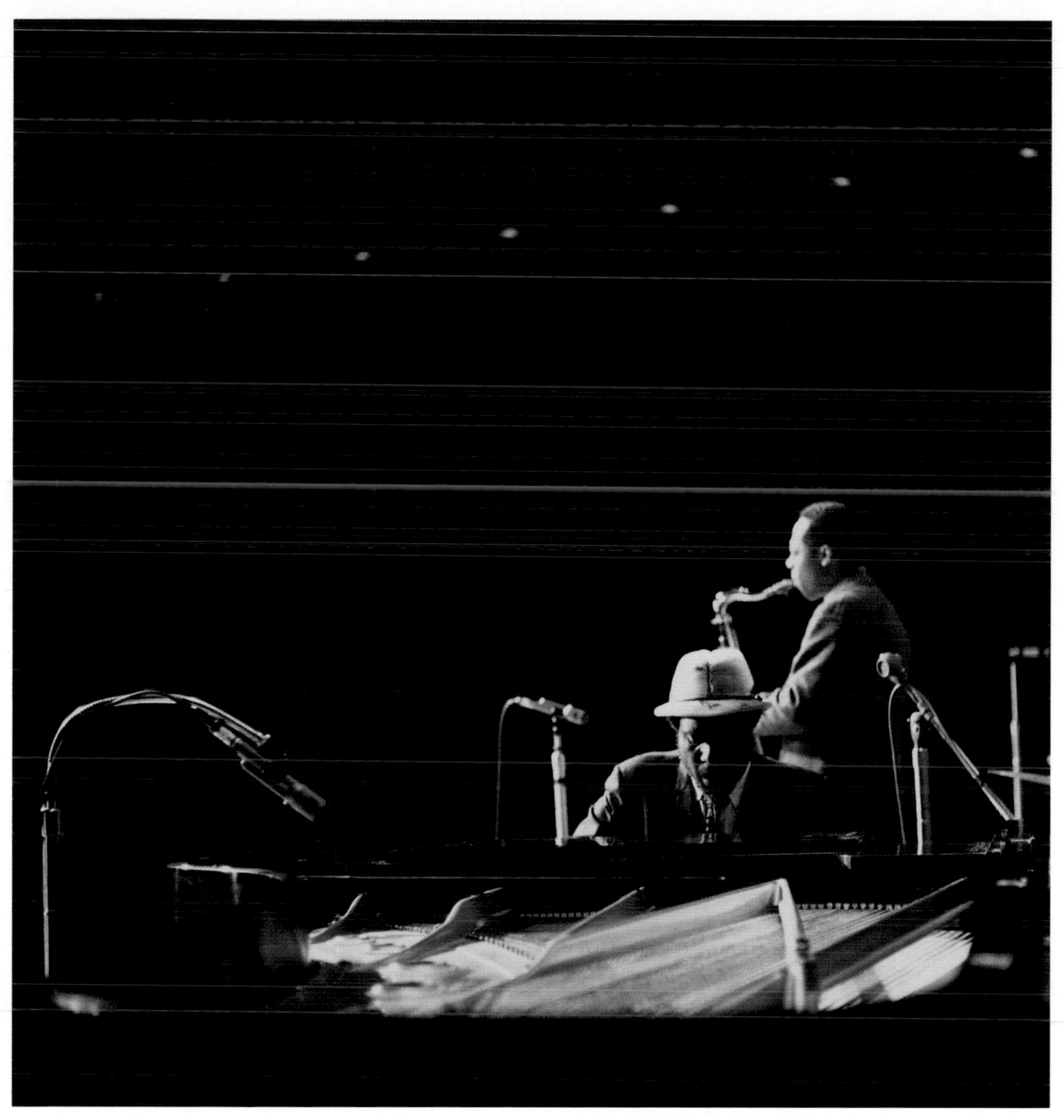

Thelonious Monk and Charlie Rouse, Boston Globe Jazz Festival, Boston, 1967

Monk remains one of the insatiably, irrepressibly and valuable individual jazzmen of our era.

—Nat Hentoff, writer

Gerry Mulligan

He brought humor back into modern jazz...a happy relaxed feeling...that permits him to play in almost any jazz context, and that makes him the big catalyst that he is.

—Gunther Schuller, composer, conductor, writer

OPPOSITE: Gerry Mulligan, Boston Globe Jazz Festival, Boston, 1967

Gerry Mulligan was very much a product of the 1940s New York scene and the big bands. He made his reputation as an arranger for Elliot Lawrence, Gene Krupa, and Claude Thornhill prior to becoming a well-respected, forceful, and imaginative instrumentalist. He was a critical figure in the Gil Evans basement apartment colloquia that included Bird, Miles Davis, Lee Konitz, John Lewis, George Russell, and John Carisi. Mulligan and Evans were the prime movers in a recasting of bebop in an organized, more relaxed, less flamboyant format—that is, a context within which subtle musical colors and textures could be heard, but without losing the necessary tension and spontaneity that makes for exceptional jazz. Their work resulted in a superb set of recordings by a nonet fronted by Miles Davis entitled *Birth of the Cool*. Nat Hentoff has commented, "Beneath the surface cool of these sessions was a great deal of concentrated intensity. At its disciplined core this too was hot jazz." This so-called cool approach was the hallmark of the future work by both Mulligan and Evans. To this extent, it was the precursor for much of what was about to develop on the West Coast, particularly in the work of Shorty Rogers and Marty Paich.

Mulligan moved to Los Angeles in 1951 and soon joined with trumpeter Chet Baker to form one of the most popular and creative small groups of the fifties. Both Mulligan and Baker were brilliant improvisers and were perfect foils for each other. Whether onstage or in the recording studio, they perfected swinging contrapuntal conversations that were on the one hand structured and well-rehearsed, but on the other hand were free expressions of the moment. This points up the apparent paradox of Mulligan himself: for all of his desire to organize—specifically with contemporary forms of jazz—he was very much an inveterate mainstream improviser whose baritone sax solos were often delightful variations on the styles of Lester Young and Coleman Hawkins. Mulligan was a great lover of the jam session. During a period in the sixties and seventies, Mulligan would sometimes show up at musical events with his horn in hand ready to play with whomever was there. If there were old-timers present, all the better. He had an abiding love and respect for the masters who had preceded him.

Mulligan moved back to the East Coast in 1953, and for the next three decades he fronted quartets, sextets, tentets, and the Concert Jazz Band, fueling them with his witty and graceful compositions. Admired by his peers and flexible in his outlook, he was delighted to create within any musical circumstance of substance. His favorite collaborators throughout the years included trumpeters Art Farmer and Clark Terry; trombonist Bob Brookmeyer; saxophonists Allen Eager, Stan Getz, Zoot Sims, Lee Konitz, Ben Webster, and Paul Desmond; pianists Dave Brubeck and Thelonious Monk; bassist Bill Crow; and drummers Dave Bailey and Mel Lewis. Unfortunately, this grand career and life were cut short too soon. As I was writing this, he died at the age of sixty-nine.

Chet Baker,
The Jazz Workshop,
Boston, 1966

He [Mulligan] had two-part inventions and fugue-like things going with Chet Baker or Bob Brookmeyer, and everything was in order. When he broke the rules, he knew what he was doing.

—George Shearing,
pianist, composer

LEFT TO RIGHT: Bob Brookmeyer, Art Farmer, and Gerry Mulligan, Newport Jazz Festival, Newport, 1963

Lee Konitz, The Jazz Workshop, Boston, 1959

Paul [Desmond] was the wittiest of improvisors. He could take a phrase that someone had played....He'd build on that phrase until he turned it inside out and seven other ways. Usually this kind of quoting is trickery, but Paul made it cohere. In his music, as in his life, the absurd cohabitated with the familiar.

—Nat Hentoff, writer

ABOVE, LEFT TO RIGHT: Paul Desmond, Dave Brubeck, and Joe Morello, Boston Globe Jazz Festival, Boston, 1967

Konitz Meets Mulligan [Capitol Records]: a simply wonderful pairing of idiosyncratic talents.

—Ron Wynn, writer

Zoot Sims,
Connolly's,
Boston,
1961

Miles Davis,
Symphony Hall,
Boston, 1968

Miles Davis

Miles Davis is a leader in jazz because he has definite confidence in what he likes and he is not afraid of what he likes...and he goes his way.

—Gil Evans, pianist, composer, arranger

The teenaged Miles Davis got his first taste of the jazz major leagues while still living in his home town of St. Louis in the summer of 1944. The powerful Billy Eckstine band was in town. Musical director Gillespie hired Davis to sit in for a trumpeter who was ill. After that Miles put aside any ideas of following his father into the dental profession and was determined to get to New York City. He did, enrolling at the Juilliard School of Music. The studies lasted for a while and had their benefits, but much of his time was spent hanging out and sitting in on jams on Fifty-second Street and at Minton's in Harlem. He worked with Coleman Hawkins, was in Benny Carter's big band, and was with the Eckstine band once again, but his first important break came when he had the opportunity to work with Bird, replacing Dizzy. Miles didn't possess the power, technical facility, or flamboyance of Dizzy or Fats Navarro. He was well aware of his limitations, however, and schooled enough to fashion a subtler style within the middle register of the trumpet. Ron Wynn described Miles' solos during this period as "carefully crafted and concise, attuned to colors and textures rather than to volume and speed." This impressionistic, understated, but evocative approach remained the basic playing style that gained him a remarkable following for his entire career.

Working around New York, Miles became a charter member of the new music seminars held in the Gil Evans West Fifty-fifth Street basement apartment. These loose group meetings resulted in a book of unique arrangements by Evans, Gerry Mulligan, John Lewis, and others that favored a subtler, slower pace, with less frenetic ensemble interaction and a performance style that called for more relaxed solos. Essentially it was a cooling down of the powerful bebop of Dizzy, Bird, and others. This approach was a reflection of Evans' and Mulligan's experiences with the style and instrumentation of the Claude Thornhill band, and it fit very well with Miles' playing style. A nine-piece group was organized that was effectively a scaled-down version of Thornhill's aggregation in that it included French horn, tuba, trumpet, trombone, and saxes. The nonet played in public only briefly, at the Royal Roost in 1948 and 1949, but it did make landmark recordings for Capitol in 1949–1950. While the band didn't survive, the musical concept did; in particular, it had subsequent though perhaps less creative incarnations on the West Coast.

Meanwhile, Miles embarked on a series of club dates and important recordings with a wide variety of New York musicians, and this activity ultimately evolved into one of the most celebrated small groups in jazz. In 1955 he had a quintet that included tenor saxist John Coltrane, pianist Red Garland, bassist Paul Chambers, and drummer Philly Joe Jones. Bill Evans replaced Garland; Evans later gave way to Wynton Kelly. Jimmy Cobb came in as the drummer, and alto saxist Cannonball Adderley joined to make the group a sextet in 1957. Nat Hentoff has said that this group ranks in importance with the Louis Armstrong Hot Fives. Their penultimate recording is titled *Kind of Blue*. During this period, Miles was also in the recording studio with arranger Gil Evans for the start of a series of magnificent large orchestral showcases of the lyrical Davis trumpet style. The first session, which produced *Miles Ahead*, was in 1957. *Porgy and Bess* followed in 1958, *Sketches of Spain* in 1960.

After the departures of Coltrane and Adderley, the sextet returned to quintet size and went through a somewhat difficult transition. One might have thought that the earlier triumphs could not be topped, but after a while Miles gathered a wholly new group together that was just as stunning. This group had tenor saxist Wayne Shorter, pianist Herbie Hancock, bassist Ron Carter, and the amazing drummer Tony Williams; this group developed a new and quite different repertoire that is best displayed on the recordings *ESP*, *Sorcerer*, and *Filles de Kilimanjaro*. The music was moving steadily away from classic bebop, with *Kilimanjaro* giving indications of the next stage of Davis' development.

The 1970s found Miles experimenting with jazz/rock/fusion. Nat Hentoff eloquently described Davis during this period as "the demonic animator of splinters of electronic sound glistening with rock, jazz, blues and his own horn of spearing loneliness." Miles expanded the quintet with pianists Chick Corea, Keith Jarrett, and Joe Zawinul; guitarist John McLaughlin; bassist Dave Holland; and drummers Jack DeJohnette, Lenny White, Billy Cobham, and others. This group made a series of provocative recordings, notably *In a Silent Way* and *Bitches Brew*. A significant byproduct of this work with Miles was that several of the musicians formed their own fusion groups.

In 1975, physically, emotionally, and artistically drained, Miles went into a self-imposed exile. The anticipated six-month break lasted for five years. When he returned he slowly regathered his earlier playing skill. As usual he surrounded himself with capable musicians, and with them played an electronic funk/rock/fusion with suspicions of jazz. I found I was not drawn to it as I had been to the earlier Davis fusion excursions. Martin Williams described rather well the frustration that an evening of listening to this group could bring: "Davis was a musician who could always come up with something so fresh, even on familiar material, as to make one forget, temporarily, all of his beautiful past. That evening everything I heard reminded me of the beautiful past with pain." In 1991, on the last lap of life in the fast lane, failing health finally caught up to Miles Davis. The beautiful past remains as a remarkable legacy.

[The Davis sextet with Coltrane, Adderley, et al.] ranks in importance with the Louis Armstrong Hot Fives.

—Nat Hentoff, writer

LEFT TO RIGHT: Cannonball Adderley, Jimmy Cobb, John Coltrane, and Miles Davis, The Chicago Amphitheater, Chicago, 1957

Wynton Kelly, Paul Chambers, and Jimmy Cobb, WGBH-TV, Boston, 1966

OPPOSITE: Miles Davis, Symphony Hall, Boston, 1968

OPPOSITE: Miles Davis and Wayne Shorter, The Jazz Workshop, Boston, 1968

Herbie Hancock, Masonic Auditorium, San Francisco, 1995

I gained a lot of freedom working with Miles Davis and also a sense of responsibility....Every time we went up there we had to be in charge of that freedom. [Miles would say,] "Long as everybody can hold up their end." In other bands that didn't even exist.

—Wayne Shorter, saxophonist, composer

Tony Williams, Kimball's East, Emeryville, California, 1993

Sonny Rollins,
The Jazz Workshop,
Boston, 1963

His music is human and stylish and warm and intense and lucid and funny and fecund and, finally, ecstatic and deeply moving.

—Gary Giddins,
writer

Sonny Rollins

A saxophone colossus.

—**Bob Altschuler, record producer**

Sonny Rollins has an imposing physical presence that matches his playing, which is at its essence a deliberate creative process. He is a singular and independent individual. As a youngster Sonny first listened to blues guitarist-singers and then discovered rhythm and blues altoist Louis Jordan, who became his link from the blues to jazz. Coleman Hawkins was Sonny's first and enduring idol and role model. Rollins patterned his tenor playing after Hawkins and later developed a synthesis with what he learned from listening to Charlie Parker. As a teenager Sonny was fortunate to find his way into the informal school and rehearsal sessions that Thelonious Monk hosted in his apartment on the West Side of Manhattan. These sessions were a seminal experience because Sonny learned how to deal with difficult music. Monk was impressed with Sonny's progress, gave him solid encouragement, and lectured him on the merits of being true to himself musically.

Sonny made his first recordings with Bud Powell and then with Miles Davis in the early 1950s. In 1954 he replaced Harold Land in the superb Max Roach/Clifford Brown quintet. Sonny stayed with Max after Brown's death, until Max disbanded in 1956. From 1956 to 1959 Sonny made a series of excellent recordings including his *Freedom Suite*, *Saxophone Colossus*, *Way Out West*, and a wonderful blowing session with Dizzy Gillespie and Sonny Stitt called *The Eternal Triangle*. A bit overwhelmed, he then dropped out for several years to refuel physically, emotionally, and intellectually—and to contemplate his future. When Sonny returned to the scene in 1961, he joined with guitarist Jim Hall for what many believe to be his finest group. Sonny and Jim interacted beautifully and Jim was an ideal foil for Sonny's ever-present sense of humor. He continued to play in public and record until 1966 and then once again went into exile, this time for five years. He returned in fine form and has been a dynamic presence on the jazz scene ever since. A live show by Sonny Rollins is very much a tour-de-force. His solos are often boiling, churning, stream-of-consciousness excursions through melody after melody that somehow all hang together beautifully and sensibly. Gary Giddins, describing one such performance, said, "Rollins made spur-of-the-moment dialectics, puns, and fluid transitions an ongoing reality....pieces weren't merely played, they were shaped....He toys with quotations....the most interesting go beyond humor and acerbity to extend the development of an idea."

Sonny Rollins, The Jazz Workshop, Boston, 1963

Coleman Hawkins and Sonny Rollins,
Newport Jazz Festival, Newport, 1963

Art Blakey

If you pass through life without hearing this music, you've missed a great deal.

—Art Blakey, drummer, bandleader, teacher

Blakey entered the early bop scene when he joined Billy Eckstine and provided an explosive driving rhythm to the latter's pioneering band of the mid-1940s. He worked around New York, with Monk, Parker, Gillespie, Clifford Brown, and others; had a seventeen-piece rehearsal band called the Messengers; and traveled to Africa to connect with his roots. Then in 1955, Blakey and Horace Silver formed the first edition of the Jazz Messengers. Blakey then took over when Silver left, and so began the nearly four-decade-long tenure of the ultimate traveling academy of contemporary small-band jazz. It was the prototype hard bop ensemble, playing exciting, aggressive blues-based material—an ideal setting for new young players who were given the opportunity to get playing experience and find their own voices before moving out on their own. Blakey's academy has had a remarkable alumni list: Donald Byrd, Benny Golson, Jackie McLean, Lee Morgan, Freddie Hubbard, Wayne Shorter, the Harper brothers, the Marsalis brothers, Benny Green, Bobby Watson, Keith Jarrett, Johnny Griffin, and many more. Blakey gloried in the success of his training program. He also found time to continue to record with Monk, Coltrane, the MJQ, and a summit of African and Latin drummers.

Lee Morgan, The Jazz Workshop, Boston, 1968

OPPOSITE: Art Blakey, WGBH-TV, Boston, 1962

OPPOSITE: Bobby Timmons, Connolly's, Boston, 1963

Joe Henderson, Monterey Jazz Festival, Monterey, 1995

Donald Byrd, Connolly's, Boston, 1961

Freddie Hubbard and Curtis Fuller, The Jazz Workshop, Boston, 1961

OPPOSITE: Freddie Hubbard, The Jazz Workshop, Boston, 1962

Curtis Fuller and Freddie Hubbard, The Jazz Workshop, Boston, 1962

Milt Jackson

> Milt did for the vibes what Dizzy did for the trumpet. He revolutionized its approach...changed its vibrato and perfected slow, cleverly paced blues solos...with long sustained notes and darting rhythms [that] became a bop staple.
>
> —Ron Wynn, writer

Milt Jackson, Kimball's East, Emeryville, California, 1992

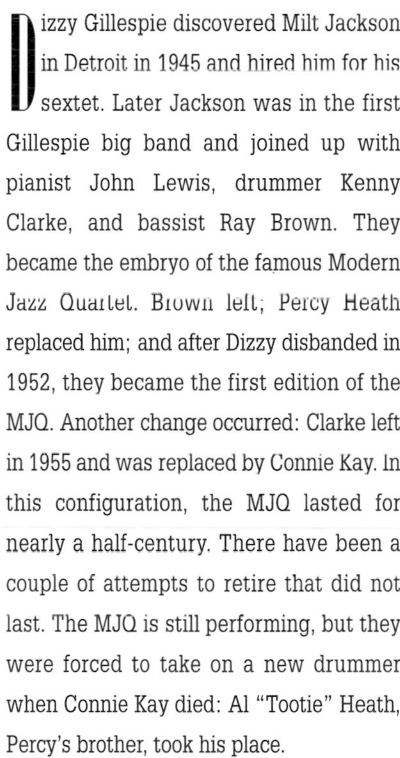

Dizzy Gillespie discovered Milt Jackson in Detroit in 1945 and hired him for his sextet. Later Jackson was in the first Gillespie big band and joined up with pianist John Lewis, drummer Kenny Clarke, and bassist Ray Brown. They became the embryo of the famous Modern Jazz Quartet. Brown left; Percy Heath replaced him; and after Dizzy disbanded in 1952, they became the first edition of the MJQ. Another change occurred: Clarke left in 1955 and was replaced by Connie Kay. In this configuration, the MJQ lasted for nearly a half-century. There have been a couple of attempts to retire that did not last. The MJQ is still performing, but they were forced to take on a new drummer when Connie Kay died: Al "Tootie" Heath, Percy's brother, took his place.

The MJQ has thrived on being a combination of rather diverse personalities and playing styles, but at all times maintaining a distinct cohesiveness. The musical content and direction have been in Lewis' hands since the outset. He carefully balanced the formal prearranged score with improvisation, integrating discipline and spontaneity. The beautiful ensemble sound of the MJQ is instantly recognizable because of the characteristic sound of Jackson's vibraphone. As soloists, Milt Jackson and John Lewis are remarkable and remarkably different. Milt is a rhapsodic melodist with amazing technique and a soulful elegance. Jackson has said regarding his style, "What is soul in jazz? It's what comes from inside....in my case, I think it's what I heard and felt in the music in my church. That was the most important influence of my career. [My style]...well it came from the church." Lewis on the other hand is brevity personified. Whitney Balliett has said that John is as lyrical a player as Milt, but he implies his lyricism, while Jackson broadcasts his.

Between the MJQ appearances, Jackson has always found time to play and record with so many of his contemporaries: Monk, Bird, Dizzy, Coltrane, Ray Charles, Ray Brown, Basie, and Wes Montgomery, as well as maintain a solo career of his own.

OPPOSITE: Milt Jackson, The Jazz Workshop, Boston, 1964

Modern Jazz Quartet, Boston Globe Jazz Festival, Boston, 1967

Max Roach

> Max, hands down, is one of the greatest soloists of all time....Max plays musical lines with dynamics and space. What he doesn't play is just as important as what he does play.
>
> **—Kenny Washington, drummer**

Max Roach was involved in the beginnings of bebop on Fifty-second Street and in Harlem literally a half-step behind such pioneers as drummer Kenny Clarke. It became evident early on that Max was destined to become the most innovative of all the new percussionists. His early influences were Jo Jones, Sid Catlett, and Chick Webb, and Max soon began to emulate Clarke's approach as well. As a teenager, he sat in with the Duke Ellington band briefly, and he played with Coleman Hawkins to make tuition for his daytime studies at the Manhattan School of Music. Dizzy got him his first recording job. As he was heard from more and more, he quickly became the bop drummer of choice, working on Fifty-second Street and recording often. Today, Max is generally considered to be the best timekeeper and improvisational foil that Charlie Parker ever had. He began fronting his own bands, leading to a brilliant but short-lived collaboration with trumpeter Clifford Brown (Brown and pianist Richie Powell were killed in an auto accident in 1956). Devastated by their deaths, Roach nonetheless continued to play, drawing on Sonny Rollins for both musical and emotional support.

As Max moved into the 1960s, he entered a new stage of his career. He was now composing extended suites, and he became an outspoken social and political activist for racial justice. In *We Insist!: Freedom Now Suite*, Max deals with his African-American heritage, African musical culture, the agonies of slavery and discrimination, and the liberation struggles in South Africa. The music (with lyrics by Oscar Brown, Jr.) and the voices, both instrumental and human, are soul-wrenching. Singer Abbey Lincoln (who was Roach's wife at the time), trumpeter Booker Little, trombonist Julian Priester, Coleman Hawkins, and Roach outdo themselves in what became a landmark statement of the very beginning of the American civil rights movement. Lincoln has become a prominent jazz singer on her own since. Linda Dahl has said, "Over the years she went from a primarily angry voice of protest to a more relaxed communicator of her feelings of dignity as a black woman and artist."

Roach continued to develop as the foremost percussion melodist in jazz. He recorded with a wide variety of musicians including avant-gardists Cecil Taylor, Archie Shepp, and Anthony Braxton. In the 1970s he organized a percussion ensemble, M'Boom, that still performs. Roach is also a faculty member at the University of Massachusetts, where he teaches master classes in drumming; received the prestigious MacArthur Foundation Fellowship in 1993; and performs regularly with his quartet, which includes trumpeter Cecil Bridgewater, tenor saxist Odean Pope, and bassist Tyrone Brown. The quartet often joins the Uptown String Quartet, which includes his violinist daughter Maxine, to perform as the Double Quartet. In 1991, Roach recorded a glorious celebration of his career accomplishments, *To The Max!*, featuring M'Boom, the Double Quartet, a choral group, and a full orchestra.

Max Roach, Kimball's East, Emeryville, California, 1991

Cecil Bridgewater, Kimball's East, Emeryville, California, 1991

Odean Pope, Kimball's East, Emeryville, California, 1991

Abbey Lincoln, Newport Jazz Festival, Newport, 1965

Horace Silver, Storyville, Boston, 1958

Horace Silver

All good music has healing potential.

—Horace Silver, pianist, composer

Blue Mitchell, Junior Cook, and Horace Silver, Storyville, Boston, 1958

Junior Cook, WGBH-TV, Boston, 1968

Horace moved to New York City from Hartford after his first road experience with Stan Getz in 1950. He soon connected with Art Blakey and they had a coop band from 1953 to 1955, which was the origin of the Jazz Messengers that Blakey took over when Horace went out on his own. Theirs was the hard bop, or soul music, style of the East Coast, which combined elements of gospel and rhythm and blues. It was often said that hard bop was a muscular, angry reaction to the largely sterile, cool school flourishing at that time on the West Coast that was led by some veterans of the 1940s bands of Kenton, Herman, and Raeburn. "No," Silver told interviewer Ben Sidran, "it just happened." That is, this was just a way of playing that developed naturally among the New York musicians, evolving from what was played in the earlier days at Minton's and on Fifty-second Street. Horace was initially influenced by Bud Powell and Monk, and was a regular visitor to the informal seminars held at Monk's apartment on West Sixty-third Street. Horace soon formulated a playing and composing style that was distinctive and infectious. Tunes like "The Preacher," "Opus de Funk," "Senor Blues," "Sister Sadie," and "Doodlin'" quickly became jazz repertoire standards and earned Horace more commercial popularity.

Horace's first and favorite quintet was together for seven years. It included Blue Mitchell on trumpet, Junior Cook on tenor sax, Gene Wright on bass, and Louis Hayes on drums (the latter replaced by Roy Brooks). Later, the front-line horn duos of his quintets were Woody Shaw and Joe Henderson, Art Farmer and Clifford Jordan, the Brecker brothers, and Tom Harrell and Bob Berg—all of whom contributed to Horace's impressive, long, and creative career (which is far from over and has recently taken on a spiritual theme).

Stan Getz and Gary Burton, WBZ-TV, Boston, 1963

Stan Getz

[In 1945, after hearing Stan for the first time, Lester Young told him:] "Nice eyes, Prez. Carry on." [In 1977, shortly before he died, Young praised him again, saying,] "You're my singer."

—**Don Maggin, writer**

In 1947, Woody Herman's composer/arranger Ralph Burns wrote "Epilogue," the final section of his *Summer Sequence Suite*. Woody assigned the solo part to his new, twenty-year-old, baby-faced saxophonist Stan Getz. Getz interpreted it so beautifully that Burns reworked the piece (now retitled "Early Autumn") to be a gorgeous showcase for him. This ballad rendition, as well as his driving Lester Youngish solos on "Four Brothers" made Stan an instant star. Getz has said that he learned his ballad style from Jack Teagarden. Clearly, Getz also listened intently to his sax section-mate Herbie Steward, who had already synthesized Lester "Prez" Young's sound and style with his own. Stan's connection to the "Prezian mode" was most obvious when he first went out on his own. With time, his sound became more full and robust. It is fascinating to listen to the 1949 recordings *The Brothers*, with Getz, Sims, Cohn, Brew Moore, and Allen Eager and note that—despite the obvious influence of Young—each had his own voice. If you compare these performances with more recent recordings, you'll hear how much each musician had matured.

Stan always had a real knack for finding accomplished collaborators. During the early period they were pianists Al Haig and Horace Silver and guitarists Jimmy Raney and Johnny Smith. In the late 1950s Stan became a part of Norman Granz's recording and touring jam session organization, joining Dizzy Gillespie, J.J. Johnson, Lionel Hampton, Roy Eldridge, Gerry Mulligan, Herb Ellis, and others. With his great technical dexterity and his wonderful feeling for the blues, Stan more than held his own.

The coming of the 1960s brought big changes. He and guitarist Charlie Byrd discovered Brazilian music, and Stan embarked on a "samba holiday" for about five years. Over the next two decades there were a long string of breathtaking collaborations with vibist Gary Burton and pianists Chick Corea, Bill Evans, Jimmy Rowles, JoAnne Brackeen, Jim McNeely, and, in the final days of Stan's life, Kenny Barron. This last collaboration was particularly special. As I listen to the tenor/piano interplay with Barron on *People Time* I find it quite reminiscent of the energy and creativity of the Louis Armstrong/Earl Hines duos of fifty years earlier.

Charlie Byrd, WBZ-TV, Boston, 1965

Chick Corea, WBZ-TV, Boston, 1968

Jim Hall

> A grace and inventiveness and lyricism that make him preeminent among contemporary guitarists.
>
> —**Whitney Balliett, writer**

Originally from Cleveland, guitarist Jim Hall made his debut with the tightly structured Chico Hamilton chamber quintet that rose out of the West Coast jazz scene of the fifties. One relaxed pick-up recording session, entitled *Grand Encounter*—with Hamilton, the MJQ's pianist and bassist (John Lewis and Percy Heath, respectively), and tenor saxist Bill Perkins—really showed the promise of Hall's emerging style. He then moved to looser, more interactive contexts with clarinetist Jimmy Guiffre and trombonist Bob Brookmeyer, exploring more traditional material.

Settling in New York City, Hall studied, experimented, and further developed his style. Drawing from guitarists Charlie Christian, Django Reinhardt, and his contemporary Jimmy Raney, he achieved a subtle, gentle virtuosity that displayed sheer harmonic magic. Hall continued to seek out and find like-minded artists, embarking on a series of brilliant collaborations over the next several decades with Art Farmer, Sonny Rollins, Lee Konitz, Ben Webster, Bill Evans, Ron Carter, Steve Swallow, Red Mitchell, and Paul Desmond. An excellent example of these collaborations is on the recording entitled *Concierto* with pianist Roland Hanna, saxist Paul Desmond, and trumpeter Chet Baker. Whitney Balliett quoted Hall: "When I play behind Paul, it becomes a question-and-answer thing between us; but all you're trying to do is swing, and swinging is a question of camaraderie." Today, he continues this same course with younger musicians. "Working with the same group all the time is nice in a lot of ways," says Jim, "but running into new people musically is stimulating. It's the newness of the encounters." As a result we can now hear some marvelous duets with Joe Lovano (tenor sax), Mike Stern and Bill Frisell (guitars), Tom Harrell (flugelhorn), and Gil Goldstein (accordion) on Jim's latest recording, *Dialogues*.

OPPOSITE: Jim Hall, The Jazz Workshop, Boston, 1960

Art Farmer and Roy Haynes, WGBH-TV, Boston, 1967

ABOVE: Jimmy Giuffre, The Jazz Workshop, Boston, 1964

LEFT: Steve Swallow, WGBH-TV, Boston, 1966

Julian and Nat Adderley

From the time I was four, my dad, a trumpet player, used to take me to see the bands....Coleman Hawkins was in the Fletcher Henderson band...he was the most interesting jazz musician I've ever seen. He just looked so authoritative. I said, 'Well that's what I want to be when I grow up.'

—**Julian Adderley, alto saxophonist**

Nat Adderley, Storyville, Boston, 1958

Saxophonist Julian "Cannonball" Adderley and his cornetist brother, Nat, fortunately survived the (unfortunate) hype that heralded their arrival in New York City in 1955 from Florida. When Cannon first played in public, there were some observers on the scene who viewed him as the second coming of Bird (who had just died). The brothers were somewhat green but extremely capable. Both went on to build solid reputations: Cannon with the Miles Davis group that included John Coltrane and Bill Evans, Nat with J.J. Johnson and the Woody Herman band. Matured, experienced, and ready in 1959, they put their own small band on the road, a tenure that lasted until Cannon's death in 1975. Joined by pianists Bobby Timmons, Victor Feldman, and Joe Zawinul and saxists Charles Lloyd and Yusef Lateef, the Adderley brothers built a solid repertoire of gospel and blues-based compositions that often incorporated just the right formula—that is, they created hits without sacrificing their musical integrity, in order to gain wide audience appeal.

OPPOSITE: Julian "Cannonball" Adderley, WGBH-TV, Boston, 1965

Julian and Nat Adderley

OPPOSITE, LEFT TO RIGHT: Nat Adderley, Cannonball Adderley, and Charles Lloyd, WGBH-TV, Boston, 1965

Bobby Timmons and J.J. Johnson, The Gilded Cage, Boston, 1963

Yusef Lateef and Nat Adderley, The Tic-Toc, Boston, 1963

Gretsch

Chico Hamilton

I'm constantly introduced to young talented players. They want to play with me because they know they'll get a chance to play...to develop. I got help when I was coming up...I'm just trying to give something back.

—Chico Hamilton, drummer, composer

OPPOSITE: Chico Hamilton, Sadao Watanabe, and Gabor Szabo, WGBH-TV, Boston, 1965

Like the young Max Roach, the teenaged Hamilton had the opportunity to sit in with Duke Ellington for a week's engagement, and did well enough to travel with the band for its California tour in the early 1940s. It was quite an experience for Chico because this was the excellent crew that included many legendary players: bassist Jimmy Blanton, saxists Ben Webster and Johnny Hodges, and trumpeters Cootie Williams and Rex Stewart. Later, Chico became the house drummer at Billy Berg's club in Hollywood (during the 1940s), toured briefly with Lionel Hampton and Lester Young, and was Lena Horne's backup drummer from the late 1940s to mid-1950s. He then became an integral part of the popular Gerry Mulligan piano-free quartet with trumpeter Chet Baker. Hamilton's next move was to organize his own group, a quintet using unusual instrumentation and exceptional musicians that included Buddy Collette (flute and reeds), Fred Katz (cello), and Jim Hall (guitar). Later editions of the quintet were just as heavily populated with stars-to-be; Hamilton had an acute ear for recognizing exceptional musicianship in young performers. Consequently, he gave important experience and exposure to reed and flute players Charles Lloyd, Eric Dolphy, Paul Horn, Sadao Watanabe, and Arthur Blythe; bassist Ron Carter; and guitarists Gabor Szabo and Larry Coryell.

Charles Lloyd and Paul Motian, WGBH-TV, Boston, 1968

Gabor Szabo, The Jazz Workshop, Boston, 1967

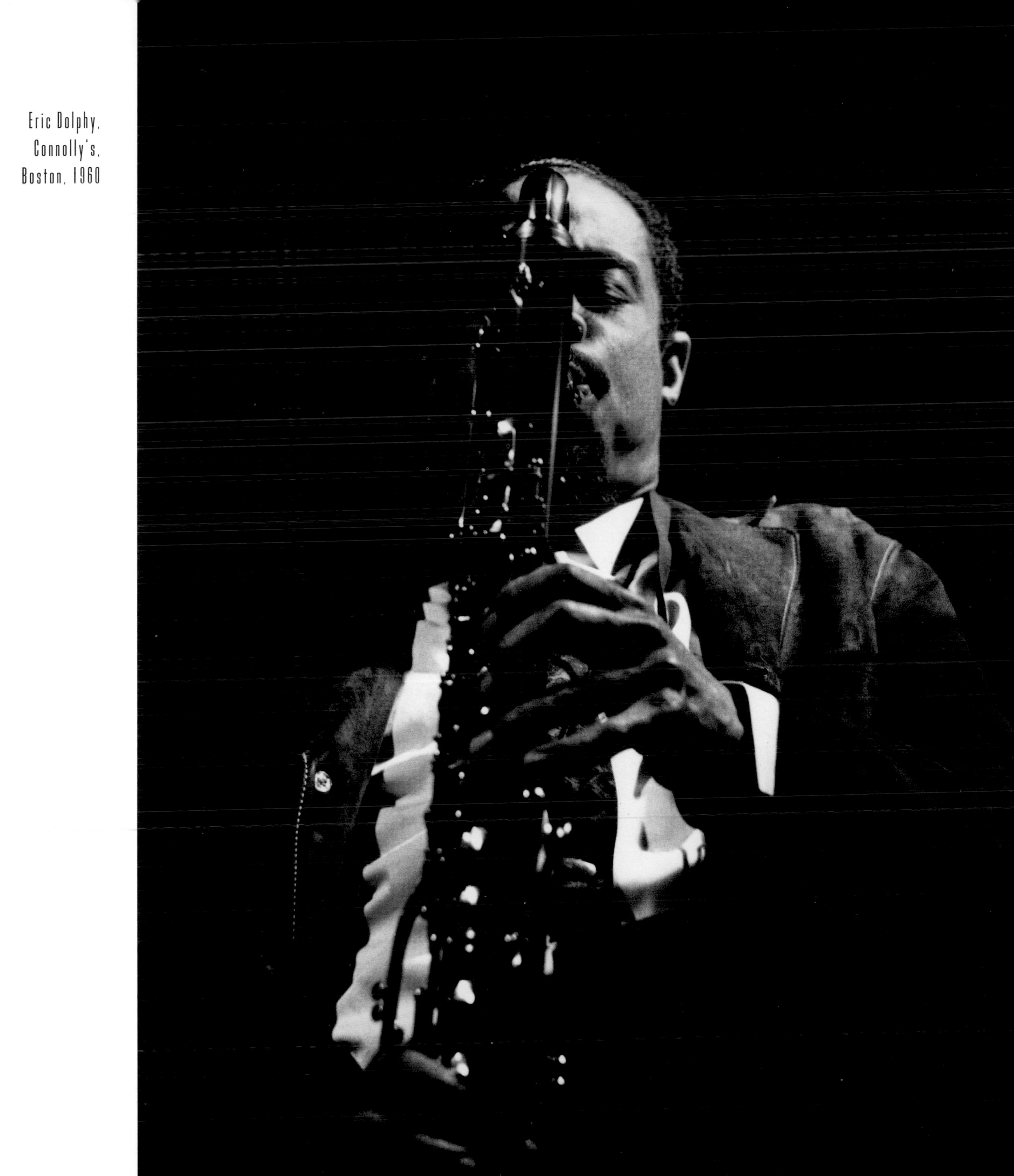

Eric Dolphy,
Connolly's,
Boston, 1960

John Coltrane,
WGBH-TV,
Boston, 1963

John Coltrane

He plays with a hard tone in a dynamically rushing style as if he might be angry. His was not an angry voice...it was the spiritual intensity.

—Ralph Gleason, writer

John Coltrane worked with several bands—Gillespie's, Earl Bostic's, and Johnny Hodges'—from 1949 to 1955 before being hired by Miles Davis for what would be a watershed experience for both of them. In 1956, struggling with drug addiction, Coltrane had to drop out temporarily to recover. On returning, he worked briefly with Thelonious Monk, and Coltrane learned a great deal. As was Monk's way, he gave Coltrane the same solid support and encouragement he gave Sonny Rollins. Coltrane rejoined Miles in 1957 and was now a greatly improved player, with better technique, a greater understanding of harmony, and a fiercely searching improvisational style. He became an integral part of one of the finest small bands in jazz history. With this new sense of himself, he began recording on his own. "Coltrane possessed one of the greatest compositional minds in jazz," said Rutgers professor Lewis Porter. "The sense of structure not only comes through in his writing and arranging, but in his improvising....His adoption of tonally slow-moving, or stationary modal jazz pieces was related to his search for more structure in his own improvisations."

By 1960, Coltrane's stature and popularity reached a high point and he decided to form his own group. During the next five years, he had the superb support of musicians he was already very much in sync with: pianist McCoy Tyner, bassist Jimmy Garrison, and drummer Elvin Jones, whose rhythmic complexity often bordered on chaos. This period culminated with the triumphant tone poem *A Love Supreme*, which summed up the spiritual growth and change that Coltrane had experienced and gloried in. He said in the liner notes, "May we never forget that in the sunshine of our lives, through the storm and after the rain—it is all with God—in all ways and forever." This period also produced superb recordings of ballads, including a special pairing of Coltrane with singer Johnny Hartman. This was an artistic accomplishment comparable to the classic 1930s recordings of Billie Holiday with Prez accompanying.

The quartet disbanded and the remaining few years of Coltrane's life were devoted to working with avant-garde musicians and experimenting with still freer methods of playing. He died in 1967.

Elvin Jones, WGBH-TV, Boston, 1966

To me he [Coltrane] was like an angel on earth. He struck me that deeply.

—Elvin Jones, drummer

[The Hartman/Coltrane recordings are] a lyric collection of beautiful ballads in which Coltrane is completely subordinate to the vocal performance of Hartman.

—Ralph Gleason, writer

Johnny Hartman, WGBH-TV, Boston, 1966

Jimmy Garrison, WGBH-TV, Boston, 1963

That [Coltrane] group was like four pistons in an engine. We were all working together to make the car go.

—McCoy Tyner, pianist

McCoy Tyner, WGBH-TV, Boston, 1964

Zoot Sims,
Connolly's,
Boston, 1961

The Tenors

> There's an apocryphal story that Adolph Sax invented the saxophone with Coleman "Bean" Hawkins in mind.
>
> —source unknown

Coleman Hawkins brought the tenor saxophone to center stage with a direct, swaggering, robust approach to melodic interpretation. He was the dominant figure in jazz until Lester Young arrived on the Kansas City scene in the '30s. Prez Young certainly acknowledged Hawkins' preeminence: "He's the person who woke you up and let you know there was a tenor saxophone." However, he proceeded to produce a creative revolution with a light, flowing, lyrical approach; he literally floated over the chords and the beat. Young's followers were dedicated. Brew Moore declared that "anybody who doesn't play like Prez is wrong!"

During the '40s Dexter Gordon was a section mate of Gene Ammons and Sonny Stitt in the great Billy Eckstine band, and later joined Illinois Jacquet and Johnny Griffin in Lionel Hampton's sax section. All have had successful solo careers and quite often one or another would pair off and take part in marvelously exciting dueling sessions, some of which fortunately were recorded. Zoot Sims and Al Cohn (both Prez-influenced people) made a career of "singing and dancing" together. Whitney Balliett once wrote that Al and Zoot breathed each other's air, and could probably, if the need arose, play each other's solos. The same could be said for the team of Eddie "Lockjaw" Davis and Johnny Griffin. Often, however, theirs was a muscular, magnetic, no-holds-barred clash onstage.

Sam Rivers was the featured soloist with the Herb Pomeroy band in Boston in the 1950s. After a short stint with Miles Davis, Sam settled into the avant-garde loft-jazz scene in lower Manhattan. Another dedicated avant-gardist is Archie Shepp. On ballads, Shepp reveals a rather romantic persona of the Ben Webster type. Archie is also a superb interpreter of the blues and gospel music, as revealed in his collaborations with pianist Horace Parlen. Coltrane-influenced Gato Barbieri started out an avant-gardist and then moved to explore his Latin American roots and jazz-rock fusion.

Sam Rivers, Connolly's, Boston, 1958

OPPOSITE: Illinois Jacquet, WGBH-TV, Boston, 1966

He [Jacquet] was all of nineteen when he started a chain reaction with his solo on Lionel Hampton's record of "Flying Home." That solo brash and swaggering served notice that something new in tenor sax stylings had been forged. There isn't a tenor player...who doesn't know that solo by heart.

—Dan Morgenstern, jazz historian, writer

Gato Barbieri, Kimball's East, Emeryville, California, 1993

Eddie "Lockjaw" Davis and Johnny Griffin, Peps, Philadelphia, 1956

Either your instrument handles you or you handle the instrument. You're not tripping through the tulips with it.

—"Lockjaw" Davis, saxophonist

OPPOSITE: Dexter Gordon, Connolly's, Boston, 1965

I like the word "jazz." That word has been my whole life. I understand the cats when they take exception to the name...But to me, that's my whole life.

—Dexter Gordon, saxophonist

Archie Shepp, Berkeley Jazz Festival, Berkeley, California, 1987

I was very fortunate....I was among a number of young people in whom he [Coltrane] took an active interest.

—Archie Shepp, saxophonist, composer

Ernie Watts, WGBH-TV, Boston, 1965

Charles Mingus

He packed his music so full of life, so full of the noise of the city, that thirty years in the future someone listening to 'Pithecanthropus Erectus' or any other wild steamrolling thing, wouldn't be sure whether that wail and scream was a horn on the record or the red-and-white siren of a prowl car shrieking past the window.

—Geoff Dyer, writer

The first time I saw Charles Mingus was about 1946 at an NBC radio studio in Rockefeller Center. He and Earl May were bassists with the Lionel Hampton band and to my great good fortune the band played his virtuoso tour-de-force "Mingus Fingers." The next time I saw him was several years later at Bop City with the amazing Red Norvo trio. The complex interactions between Mingus, vibist Norvo, and guitarist Tal Farlow were astonishing to hear. Unfortunately, the trio was short-lived because Mingus had a hassle related to a television appearance. Mingus is as well known for his mercurial nature as for his musical prowess.

My next in-person experience was with the Mingus Jazz Workshop on one of those wonderful evenings when the performances were just right. I was in the audience at the Downbeat in Philadelphia in 1956 when the group had saxists Jackie McLean and J.R. Montrose and pianist Mal Waldron. Mingus was joyously delighted as they played "A Foggy Day" and "Pithecanthropus Erectus," both just recorded for Atlantic. On another evening, however, when Charles' life was in a deep funk (he and trombonist Jimmy Knepper had just clashed), Mingus was introduced to me by bassist John Neves and we became club-hopping companions, going from Birdland to the Half Note. At the Half Note we shared tables with dancer Katherine Dunham and her friends, people neither of us knew. Later, we were invited to her place at the Chelsea Hotel, but I was soon caught in the midst of a near-debacle because of Charles' unpleasant mood. I was politely asked to take my friend elsewhere. Once on the street, Charles became docile and apologetic. We drove around the city for hours of delightful conversation and I then dropped him off in Harlem as the sun was coming up. He apparently made his peace with Dunham, since I heard they had subsequently worked together.

Mingus, like his lifelong idol Ellington and Thelonious Monk, built a grand repertoire of his own music. He hired musicians whom he sensed would represent the music as he felt it; he wanted his sound from each instrument and from the ensemble. Within this context he also encouraged his players to develop their own things to express. If it all didn't work out, Charles would not hesitate to let someone go on the spot, even during a performance. Nat Hentoff quoted one of his former players: "He just wouldn't let you coast." Over the years, such instrumentalists as saxists Booker Ervin, Eric Dolphy, Rahsaan Roland Kirk, and Charlie Mariano; pianists Jaki Byard and Toshiko Akiyoshi; trombonist Jimmy Knepper; his dependable rhythm driver, drummer Danny Richmond; and many others were able to satisfy his desires.

Mingus was constantly developing his ideal: a collective group interaction and counterpoint. Often the music wasn't written out. He would play the individual parts on the piano and get the musicians to commit them to memory, his goal being to maintain a sense of spontaneity. There was a storm within this man—a great frustration stirred within an enormous heart that cared deeply about the human condition and the giving and receiving of love...and it all came out in his music. His output was often deeply rooted in the music and styles of the past, and he enjoyed celebrating such past greats as Lester Young, Ellington, and Jelly Roll Morton with musical tributes. His last years were difficult because the debilitating muscular disease ALS (also known as Lou Gehrig's disease) made it impossible for him to move about or play, but he directed several fine recordings from a wheelchair up to 1978. He died in Mexico in 1979. An alumni group, Mingus Dynasty, often performed his music after his death.

Recently, Gunther Schuller and associates gathered and orchestrated Mingus' vast unfinished work *Epitaph* and, with a large orchestra that includes many Mingus alumni, performed it several times, including once in New York City's Lincoln Center and once in San Francisco's Davies Symphony Hall. They also made a recording. Several years ago Mingus Dynasty and the *Epitaph* orchestra evolved into the Mingus Big Band, which at this writing performs a once-a-week tribute to Mingus at Manhattan's Time Cafe. It is one of the finest bands I have ever heard...exuberant, explosive, and spontaneous.

OPPOSITE: Charles Mingus, The Five Spot, New York, 1962

Rahsaan
Roland Kirk,
Boston Globe Jazz
Festival, Boston,
1967

Booker Ervin, Connolly's,
Boston, 1958

Roland Kirk might spin a bass on top of his head, but that bass is in tune.

—Charles Mingus, bassist, composer

Charlie Mariano, Connolly's, Boston, 1962

Eric Dolphy,
Connolly's,
Boston, 1960

Jackie McLean, Connolly's, Boston, 1962

This human thing in instrumental playing has to do with trying to get as much human warmth and feeling into my work as I can. I want to say more on my horn than I ever could in ordinary speech.

—Eric Dolphy, reed player

Jaki Byard, WGBH-TV, Boston, 1965

Kenny Burrell, The Jazz Workshop, Boston, 1965

The Guitars

Probably every guitarist in jazz has a debt to [Charlie] Christian, who in his short life—he died in 1942 aged twenty-four—became the most important early explorer of amplified guitar as a solo instrument.

—Gene Lees, writer, lyricist, singer

The first guitarist to catch my attention was Teddy Bunn, who played an acoustic instrument. It was the early 1940s and I discovered him when I discovered Sidney Bechet (Bunn's single-string work on Sidney's classic recording of "Summertime" is marvelous). Shortly afterward I heard the amazing Charlie Christian on a set of rare recorded performances with clarinetist Edmund Hall; it was rare because Christian was playing an acoustic guitar. It wasn't until I tuned into a live radio broadcast of the Benny Goodman sextet that I heard the electrically amplified Christian. That's when I got the full impact of his remarkable facility and glorious ideas.

From the mid-forties on, jazz guitarists have been the offspring of Charlie Christian with some added measure of the French gypsy Django Reinhardt. Guitarist and teacher Jimmy Stewart said, "Charlie's use of offbeat accents and syncopation, coupled with his view that no interval is wrong, gave his music a new flexibility. He was a genius in manipulating lines. He molded his phrases so that the melodic line sometimes appeared on the second or third beat...unusual in jazz at the time." It is no wonder that he took the jazz world by storm during his very short lifetime. I was also listening to Django Reinhardt at that time; he was with the quintet of The Hot Club of France. Somebody once said (unkindly) that The Hot Club swung like a rusty gate; indeed, the chunka-chunk-chunk rhythm was (charmingly) old-fashioned. By contrast, however, it made Django's more advanced style, fleet fingering, and unique gypsy-jazz ideas all the more mind-blowing.

Les Paul's performances with pianist Nat Cole in the early Jazz at the Philharmonic concerts are excellent examples of the combined influence of Christian and Reinhardt. By the late 1940s these effects were combined with a large helping of Charlie Parker's influence to produce what Whitney Balliett described as "a sleek florid style that left no note unturned." Barney Kessell, Jimmy Raney, and Tal Farlow were among the earliest practitioners of the style. Perhaps Wes Montgomery developed the most distinctive style. Writer Tom Owens described that Montgomery's sound stemmed from the use of his thumb (rather than a pick) to pluck the strings, giving a softer, gentler attack than his contemporaries. He also played melodies in octaves with great ease. All this aside, Owens felt that Montgomery's melodic and rhythmic inventiveness made him a more than worthy member of the Christian dynasty. George Benson fits in here as well. Unfortunately, he caught the Nat Cole vocalizing bug, and you only hear Benson's fine playing occasionally.

Herb Ellis was a stalwart member of the Oscar Peterson trio and participated in many of the jam session recordings and concerts organized by Norman Granz. Ellis is at his best in a blues context. Nat Hentoff has been an avid listener because of Ellis' "depth and blues-driven swing...the joy and energy of his improvisations."

Kenny Burrell's playing is smooth and relaxed, but it is full of expression and energy. Restraint is the special ingredient in his straightforward melody lines, elegant phrasing, and mellow tone. Grant Green, in contrast, had a more aggressive approach derived from his rhythm and blues beginnings. He combined these blues roots with a mastery of bebop and a simplicity that put expressiveness ahead of technical facility. Green was a vastly underrated player when he died at the age of forty-eight.

The first strongly rock-influenced jazz guitarist was Larry Coryell. He built a wonderful reputation with the Gary Burton Quartet in the '60s before going out on his own. His collaborations with guitarists Philip Catherine, John McLaughlin, and Emily Remler are quite special.

New York City (in the '60s) represented two things: the old jazz tradition...and something new because Bob Dylan and the Beatles were happening then. I always admired rock & roll and I loved to play blues—especially string bending. But jazz was always the first priority. I never confused the musicality and the integrity of jazz with the spirit and different rhythmic infusions of rock.

—Larry Coryell, guitarist

Larry Coryell, WGBH-TV, Boston, 1967

Herb Ellis and Terry Gibbs, Kimball's East, Emeryville, California, 1991

I knew about the electric guitar before I came in contact with electric lights. We lived by candlelight and kerosene until I was seven. When we moved into a house with electricity, the first thing my stepfather did was to get his electric guitar out of the pawnshop, take it home, and plug it in. I remember waking up to that sound.

—George Benson, guitarist, singer

George Benson,
WGBH-TV,
Boston, 1969

Wes Montgomery, WGBH-TV, Boston, 1966

Wes Montgomery...played pretty for the people—without cynicism or condescension but with honesty and understanding.

—Howard Mandel, writer

OPPOSITE: Grant Green and Clifford Jarvis, WGBH-TV, Boston, 1966

Lambert, Hendricks & Ross, Columbia Recording Studios, New York, 1962

We're the "Metropolitan Bopera Company."

—Dave Lambert, singer

The Singers

I hate straight singing. I have to change a tune to my own way of doing it.

—Billie Holiday, singer

In the 1920s Louis Armstrong opened the inspirational floodgates in jazz with his playing, and his singing was just as influential. He just translated his playing style to vocalizing, exhibiting the same ease, great warmth, and impeccable phrasing of his trumpet work. He also invented scat singing, wordless imitations of instrumental sounds. "You do like the horn does," said singer Jon Hendricks. "You begin with the melody subliminally and interpret the chord structure. That's scat singing." Many jazz singers have been following Louis ever since. Actually, Ella Fitzgerald learned this fine art from Dizzy Gillespie. Her recordings of "Flying Home," "How High the Moon," and "Lady Be Good" in the mid-'40s had everybody, musicians and fans alike, absolutely astonished. Mel Tormé said, "A singer has to work doubly hard to emit those random notes in scat singing with perfect intonation. Well, I should say all singers except Ella. Her notes float out in perfect pitch, effortless and, most important of all, swinging." She then went on to become a premier interpreter of The Great American Popular Song using her warm exquisite phrasing and a sweet, honest delivery. She's a singer's singer.

In the 1950s and 1960s Jon Hendricks and his cohorts Dave Lambert and Annie Ross brought scat to a fine state of organization and perfection by using vocalese, or putting words as well as sounds to the recorded solos and ensembles of great musicians. Lambert was only half-kidding when he said, "We're the 'Metropolitan Bopera Company'." Nat Hentoff commented that they were only three but often sounded like a rambunctious big band when they performed; he also expressed the thought that there was so much infectious delight in their swinging vocation, yet they always tried to do justice to the instrumental inventions they were appropriating. Anne Marie Moss substituted for Annie Ross briefly and later performed delightful vocalese arrangements with her husband, Jackie Paris (who was also well known for his soulful singing with the Charles Mingus Jazz Workshop). Another married duo that create vocalese magnificently are Jackie Cain and Roy Kral, their performances enhanced by Kral's fine piano playing.

Two dedicated jazz singers who got their start in remarkably similar ways in the late 1940s, but in two different cities, are Sheila Jordan and Helen Merrill. A teenaged Jordan hung out at the jazz clubs in Detroit and later in New York, where she absorbed everything she heard, particularly the playing of Charlie Parker. This experience, along with classes with Lennie Tristano and encouragement from Charles Mingus, taught her to be harmonically sophisticated and to take risks with the melody line of songs. Francis Davis described it this way: "What Jordan does best is to reimagine the lyrics of faded pop standards, declaiming them over and over, in and out of tempo, sliding them up or down a quarter-tone until they begin to make sense to her." Her first break came with avant-gardist composer George Russell in the 1960s. While still very much a cult figure today, she has had her successes and is still performing.

As a teenager, Helen Merrill hung out at a club in the Bronx where many fine musicians, including Charlie Parker, played. She got together with out-of-work singers and musicians and jammed. Leslie Gourse says that Helen described it as the school of chord changes. Helen said, "We spent all our time trying to figure out new chord changes, improvising on them.... Take the chord structure, change it and call it by a different name." Eventually, she sang with Mingus and later with the Earl Hines sextet. In 1954, she made a classic recording of ballads arranged by Quincy Jones and featuring the superb accompaniment of trumpeter Clifford Brown. Describing Merrill's singing, Leslie Gourse says, "She sings down a half-tone from the written note, then again down on another note, then up a half-tone from another written note. That's how Helen Merrill on record gains control of you and handles your heart and soul with a melody." Over the years Merrill has recorded with Teddy Wilson, Bill Evans, Stan Getz, and, several times, the Gil Evans band. Her most recent recording at this writing is a tribute to Clifford Brown.

Over the years, hardworking trumpeter Jack Sheldon played with the Stan Kenton, Benny Goodman, Woody Herman, and Bill Berry big bands as well as many small groups. He also had a parallel career as a hip comedian and television personality: he was a regular foil for Merv Griffin. Jack is recognized as a capable improviser and a charming singer. He has a musician's sensibility, and his phrasing and humor are reminiscent of Jack Teagarden, Bob Dorough, Dave Frishberg, Ben Sidran, Jimmy Rowles, Woody Herman, and Joe Mooney.

Mose Allison—pianist, trumpeter, composer, and singer—is another matter. He is a special hybrid of a country-blues style singer (he's from Tippo, Mississippi) with a wry, urban sophistication (he's lived most of his life on Long Island, just outside New York City). I first heard him playing piano for Stan Getz and for the Al Cohn and Zoot Sims duo; Allison gave them a strong rollicking blues base to swing off. His first recordings on his own were of his own compositions and were called *The Back Country Suite* and *Local Color*. They are wonderful mini tone-poems, or vignettes, that reflected his rural southern background. As time went on, the songs that he wrote evolved into satirical commentaries on the dilemmas of life and on social and political absurdities. He developed an original and colorful speaking style of singing that wedded traditional blues phrasing with the classic jazz phrasing that Louis Armstrong pioneered. It effectively delivers the drama of Allison's wry, poignant, and humorous lyrics.

Sheila Jordan, Newport Jazz Festival, Newport, 1962

I had two separate reviews from the same concert...top reviewers. One said I looked great, but I didn't fulfill my capacity; in other words I didn't sing that good. The other one said I didn't look too hot but, boy could I sing.

—Sheila Jordan, singer

Jackie Cain and Roy Kral, WGBH-TV, Boston, 1966

Ella Fitzgerald, Newport Jazz Festival, Newport, 1963

Anne Marie Moss and Jackie Paris, Paul's Mall, Boston, 1965

'You've got something special,' Art Tatum said to me. I nearly flipped. I grew up in the bebop era....That experience you can't buy. The great moments of learning something every day.

—Jackie Paris, singer, guitarist

Jack Sheldon, Gabiano's, San Francisco, 1994

Helen Merrill, New York University, New York, 1977

Mose Allison,
The Atlantic
House,
Provincetown,
Massachu-
setts, 1965

Thad Jones–Mel Lewis band with Jimmy Owens as solo trumpet, Boston Globe Jazz Festival, Boston, 1967

Keepers of the Big Band Flame

Big bands comprised of trumpets, trombones, saxes and rhythm became one of the historically significant instrumentations, like the string quartet and the symphony orchestra, for one simple reason: it works.

—Gene Lees, writer, lyricist, singer

Just keeping a fifteen-to-twenty piece band together after the forties, let alone putting it on the road, was usually a losing financial proposition. However, the desire to keep large-ensemble music alive was strong enough to keep a few stalwart souls at it for more than the past forty years. Basie, Ellington, Herman, Hampton, Stan Kenton and occasionally Benny Goodman—were out there. In addition, there was "super-drummer-man" Buddy Rich and "super-horn-man" Maynard Ferguson. These two showmen were powerhouse soloists and fronted marvelous, loud, and straight-ahead swinging aggregations.

The Latin-jazz bands have remained a steady force starting with Machito's Afro-Cuban Orchestra, which often featured Dizzy Gillespie, Charlie Parker, Flip Phillips, Lee Konitz, and Howard McGee as soloists when they would play the Royal Roost and Birdland in the '40s and '50s. Master percussionist Tito Puente, who recorded with Dizzy and Woody Herman, still keeps a powerful band on the road. So does the explosive and dazzling pianist Eddie Palmieri, whose playing is strongly influenced by Thelonious Monk, McCoy Tyner, and Herbie Hancock.

Most often, the interesting and adventuresome bands were those that started out as rehearsal bands—that is, a band organized so that composer-arrangers could hear their music performed. In such a band, the personnel is usually pretty top-flight because excellent musicians working commercial jobs are anxious to do something more creative at least once a week. If they are able to stay together, these bands frequently find opportunities to perform in public, usually locally, and sometimes would travel. The quintessential example of this scenario was the band that trumpeter Thad Jones and drummer Mel Lewis fronted on Monday nights for many years at New York's Village Vanguard. Jones had been a strong performer in the 1950s Basie band, but had been quite frustrated because Basie had rarely used Jones' arrangements. The rehearsal band was the perfect showcase, and Jones-Lewis shared it with arranger and trombonist Bob Brookmeyer.

Arranger Gil Evans also organized a band, which has been fronted since his death by his son, trumpeter Miles. Maria Schneider, a composer protégé of Evans and Bob Brookmeyer, has one of the newest bands in New York City at this writing. And, of course, there is also the absolutely fabulous Mingus Big Band. In a way, it is an anti-rehearsal band: the musicians go to work each Thursday evening with an attitude and sensibility true to Mingus' workshop concept to be spontaneous and original.

Berklee College of Music faculty member Herb Pomeroy has done the same thing in Boston, drawing on many of the college staff as band members. Terry Gibbs, Bill Holman, Bill Berry, and Nat Pierce have kept bands going in the Los Angeles area; Mike Vax and Joe Henderson do it in San Francisco; and Rob McConnell has had a band going in Toronto, Canada, for twenty-five years.

Two other remarkably gifted and unique composers with similar histories are pianists Toshiko Akiyoshi and Carla Bley. Akiyoshi, who leads a band with her husband, saxophonist Lew Tabackin, brings her Asian background to bear a great deal in her compositions. She has said, "Being Japanese in the jazz world is a positive aspect in that I could draw something from my own culture and perhaps return to the jazz tradition something that might make it a little bit richer than before." Carla Bley, on the other hand, is even more eclectic, with a bent toward the humorous and satiric. Her sources of inspiration run the gamut from Kurt Weill to Ellington to British music-hall tunes to the blues, as well as to rock. At times, she is not sure her music can be defined as jazz, but with the exceptionally skilled jazz players in her band, it certainly sounds that way. Of Carla, Linda Dahl says, "Bley often uses the word outrageous in describing herself and her band. She is an entertainer who loves the absurd, but is dead serious about her music." And it shows.

Trombonist Slide Hampton was a lead arranger for Maynard Ferguson, and in the 1960s he led an octet that featured his own music. He is currently leading a very special twelve-piece repertory ensemble named the JazzMasters that is dedicated to the music of Dizzy Gillespie and Charlie Parker, with the majority of the arrangements written by Hampton.

Finally, the latest big band hero is veteran tenor sax giant Illinois Jacquet. Illinois was a teenager with Lionel Hampton's early 1940s band, famous for driving the audiences into a frenzy with his solo on "Flying Home." Much to his credit, Jacquet is now reliving the past to his great delight with an exceptional big band.

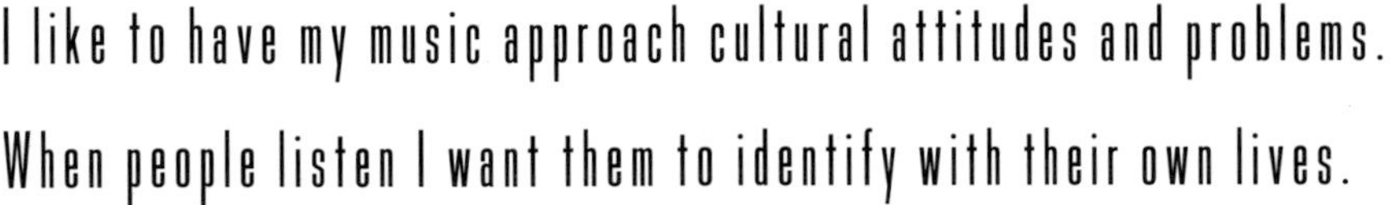

I like to have my music approach cultural attitudes and problems. When people listen I want them to identify with their own lives.

—Toshiko Akiyoshi, pianist, composer, bandleader

ABOVE: Tito Puente, Kimball's East, Emeryville, California, 1993

LEFT: Toshiko Akiyoshi, Connolly's, Boston, 1962

Carla Bley, Herbst Theater, San Francisco, 1994

Slide Hampton Octet, Connolly's, Boston, 1959

It don't mean a thing if it ain't got that swing.

—Duke Ellington, bandleader, composer, pianist

Illinois Jacquet, WGBH-TV, Boston, 1966

Reprise

A cold winter afternoon in Boston, and I, sixteen, am passing the Savoy Cafe in the black part of town. A slow blues curls out into the sunlight and pulls me indoors. Count Basie, hat on, with a half-smile, is floating the beat with Jo Jones's brushes whispering behind him. Out on the floor, sitting on a chair which is leaning back against a table, Coleman Hawkins fills the room with big deep bursting sounds, conjugating the blues with rhapsodic sweep and fervor he so loves in the opera singers whose recordings he plays by the hour at home.

The blues goes on and on as the players turn it round and round and inside out and back again, showing more of its faces than I ever thought existed. I stand inside the door, careful not to move and break the priceless sound. In a way I am still standing there.

—Nat Hentoff, writer

And so am I. Hentoff's eloquence speaks to my own early experiences in the same town, on the very same streets, years later. I seem to be back where I started, singing the praises of jazz musicians of all ages who live to be inspired to create and who just won't quit. With each year of playing, these jazz masters add to a storehouse of knowledge and experience that invariably enriches whatever they do in the future. I was delighted to read in a Peter Watrous concert review in *The New York Times* that trumpeter Nicholas Payton (in his twenties) loves the jam session. He says, "They open your ears to interaction. You can play in a way which to me embodies the creative spirit that the music is about." According to veteran saxophonist Teddy Edwards, "You trade ideas [at a jam session] and you see if you can come up to the level. Sometimes you fall short. Whatever happened, the next day you got up, put on a pot of beans and practiced all day." Watrous goes on to say, "Age in jazz can often be an indication of musical knowledge. [At an Avery Fisher Hall concert, veteran] saxophonists Von Freeman, Teddy Edwards, Johnny Griffin and Joe Lovano played with so much information and wit that the audience was left in awe of the music and not the physicality of the performance."

Photographing and listening to these wonderful musicians over the years has left me in awe, as well as deeply grateful that I had all these opportunities, and I look forward to many more in the future. Putting this book together has been extrememly fulfilling. Collecting my favorite photographs was certainly something special. However, recalling my experiences, my likes and some dislikes, and relistening to the music (quite often discovering things that I had missed the first time around) has been an unexpected pleasure provided by this project. My heartfelt thanks to all the musicians that made this such a grand lifetime experience.

OPPOSITE: Steve Swallow, Newport Jazz Festival, Newport, 1963

Bibliography

Books of Photographs

Abe, K., ed. *Jazz Giants.* New York: Billboard Publications, 1988.

______. *Fifty Jazz Greats.* Tokyo: Shinka Music Publishing Co., 1995.

Berendt, Yoachim, ed. *Jazz: A Photo History.* New York: Schirmer Books, 1979.

Bergerot, Franck, and Arnaud Merlin, eds. *The Story of Jazz—Bop & Beyond.* New York: H.N. Abrams, Inc., 1993.

Brask, Ole. *Jazz People.* New York: H.N. Abrams, Inc., 1976.

______. *Photographs.* Kiel, Germany: Nieswand Verlag, 1995.

Carles, Phillipe, and Andre Clergeat, eds. *Jazz—Les Incontournables.* Paris, France: Editions Filipacci, 1992.

Claxton, William. *Jazz.* Pasadena, Calif.: Twelvetrees, 1987.

______. *Young Chet.* Munich, Germany: Schirmer/Mosel, 1993.

______. *Claxography.* Kiel, Germany: Nieswand Verlag, 1996.

DeCarava, Roy. "A Retrospective." New York: Museum of Modern Art, 1996.

Feingold, Deborah, Bob Young, and Al Stankus. *Jazz Cooks.* New York: Stewart, Jacobi & Chang, Inc., 1992.

Friedman, Carol. *A Moment's Notice.* New York: Schirmer Books, 1983.

Friedman, Laura, and Julie Coryell. *Jazz-Rock Fusion.* New York: Delta/Dell Publishing, 1978.

Gignoux, Dany. *Dizzy Gillespie.* Kiel, Germany: Nieswand Verlag, 1993.

Gottlieb, William. *The Golden Age of Jazz.* San Francisco: Pomegranate Art Books, 1995.

Hentoff, Nat, and Robert Parent. *Jazz Is* (photos by Robert Parent). New York: Limelight Editions, 1984.

Hinton, Milt. *Bass Line.* Philadelphia: Temple University Press, 1988.

______. *Over Time.* San Francisco: Pomegranate Art Books, 1991.

Landergren, Christer. *Body & Soul.* Stockholm, Sweden: Fotographicentrums, 1987.

Leloir, Jean-Pierre, and William Gottlieb. *Jazz—Dedicated to Cool Cats.* Tokyo: G.I.P., 1991.

Leonard, Herman. *The Eye of Jazz.* New York: Viking Penguin, 1985.

______. *Jazz Memories.* Paris, France: Editions Filipacchi, 1995.

Le Querrec, Guy. *Banlieues Bleues.* Paris, France: Scandeditions, 1993.

Lowe, Jacques. *Jazz—Photographs of the Masters.* New York: Artisan, 1995.

Lyons, Len, and Veryl Oakland. *The Great Jazz Pianists* (photos by Veryl Oakland). New York: Da Capo, 1983.

Mili, Gjon. *Photographs & Recollections.* Boston: Little, Brown & Co., 1980.

Motion, Tim, ed. *An Eye for the Sound.* New York: Smithmark Publishers, Inc., 1994.

Peterson, Donald, and W. Royal Stokes, eds. *Swing Era New York—Charles Peterson's Photographs.* Philadelphia: Temple University Press, 1994.

Polonsky, Bruce. *Hearing Music.* San Francisco: Private Books, 1981.

Quinke, Ralph. *Jazz + More.* Kiel, Germany: Nieswand Verlag, 1992.

Reeves, John. *Jazz Lives.* Buffalo, N.Y.: Firefly Books, 1992.

Reiff, Carol. *Nights in Birdland.* New York: Simon & Schuster, Inc., 1987.

Sidran, Ben, and Lee Tanner. *Talking Jazz* (photos by Lee Tanner). New York: Da Capo Press, 1995.

Smith, Bill. *Imagine the Sound No. 5.* Toronto, Canada: Nightwood Editions, 1985.

Sol, Ydo. *Faces of Jazz.* Kiel, Germany: Nieswand Verlag, 1992.

Spitzer, David. *Jazz.* San Francisco: Woodford Publishing, 1994.

Steichen, Edward, ed. *The Family of Man.* New York: Museum of Modern Art, 1955.

Stewart, Charles. *Jazz Files.* Boston: Little, Brown & Co., 1985.

Stewart, Frank, and Wynton Marsalis. *Sweet Swing Blues on the Road.* New York: W.W. Norton & Co., 1994.

Stock, Dennis. *Jazz Street.* New York: Doubleday & Co., Inc., 1960.

Stoll, Jerry. *Jazz Memories.* San Francisco: Pomegranate Art Books, 1987.

Tanner, Lee, ed. *Dizzy—John Birks Gillespie in His 75th Year.* San Francisco: Pomegranate Art Books, 1992.

______. *Jazz Photographs.* San Francisco: Pomegranate Art Books, 1993.

Van der Elsken, Ed. *Jazz: 1955–1959 & 1961.* Amsterdam, The Netherlands: Fragment Uitgevrij, 1988.

Williams, Richard, ed. *Miles Davis, The Man in the Green Shirt.* New York: Henry Holt & Co. Inc., 1993.

______. *Jazz—A Photographic Documentary.* New York: Crescent Press, 1994.

Willoughby, Bob. *Jazz.* Kiel, Germany: Nieswand Verlag, 1990.

Wilmer, Valerie. *The Face of Black Music.* New York: Da Capo Press, 1976.

Wolff, Francis. *The Blue Note Years.* New York: Rizzoli International Publications, 1995.

Wulf, Ingo, ed. *Chet Baker in Europe.* Kiel, Germany: Neiswand Verlag.

Texts on Jazz

Alkyer, Frank, ed. *Down Beat—60 Years of Jazz.* Milwaukee, Wis.: Hal Leonard Corp., 1995.

Balliett, Whitney. *New York Notes.* New York: Da Capo Press, 1977.

______. *American Musicians.* New York: Oxford University Press, 1986.

______. *American Singers.* New York: Oxford University Press, 1988.

______. *Barney.* Bradley & Max. New York: Oxford University Press, 1989.

______. *Goodbyes & Other Messages.* New York: Oxford University Press, 1991.

Berendt, Yoachim. *The Jazz Book.* New York: Lawrence Hill & Co., 1975.

Britt, Stan. *Long Tall Dexter.* New York: Da Capo Press, 1989.

Carr, Ian. *Miles Davis.* New York: Quill, 1982.

Carr, Ian, Digby Fairweather, and Brian Priestly, eds. *Jazz—The Rough Guide.* London, England: The Rough Guides, 1995.

Chilton, John. *The Song of the Hawk.* Ann Arbor, Mich.: The University of Michigan Press, 1990.

Clancy, William. *Woody Herman, Chronicles of the Herds.* New York: Schirmer Books, 1995.

Cook, Richard, and Brian Morton. *The Penguin Guide to Jazz.* London, England: Penguin Books, 1992.

Crow, Bill. *Jazz Anecdotes.* New York: Oxford University Press, 1990.

______. *From Birdland to Broadway.* New York: Oxford University Press, 1992.

Crowther, Bruce, and Mike Pinfold. *The Big Band Years.* New York: Facts on File Publications, 1988.

Dahl, Linda. *Stormy Weather.* New York: Limelight Editions, 1984.

Dance, Stanley. *The World of Duke Ellington.* New York: Da Capo Press, 1970.

______. *The World of Earl Hines.* New York: Da Capo Press, 1977.

______. *The World of Swing.* New York: Da Capo Press, 1979.

Davis, Francis. *In the Moment.* New York: Oxford University Press, 1986.

______. *Outcats.* New York: Oxford University Press, 1990.

______. *Bebop & Nothingness.* New York: Schirmer Books, 1996.

Dyer, Geoff. *But Beautiful.* New York: North Point Press, 1996.

Enstice, Wayne, and Paul Rubin. *Jazz Spoken Here.* New York: Da Capo Press, 1994.

Feather, Leonard. *Inside Jazz.* New York: Da Capo Press, 1949.

______. *From Satchmo to Miles.* New York: Da Capo Press, 1972.

______. *The Jazz Years.* New York: Da Capo Press, 1987.

______. *The Passion for Jazz.* New York: Da Capo Press, 1990.

Giddens, Gary. *Riding on a Blue Note.* New York: Oxford University Press, 1981.

______. *Rhythm-A-Ning.* New York: Oxford University Press, 1985.

______. *Faces in the Crowd.* New York: Oxford University Press, 1992.

Gillespie, Dizzy. *To Be or Not to Bop.* New York: Da Capo Press, 1979.

Gioia, Ted. *West Coast Jazz.* New York: Oxford University Press, 1992.

Gitler, Ira. *Jazz Masters of the '40s.* New York: Da Capo Press, 1985.

______. *Swing to Bop.* New York: Da Capo Press, 1986.

Goldberg, Joe. *Jazz Masters of the '50s.* New York: Da Capo Press, 1983.

Gordon, Max. *Live at the Village Vanguard.* New York: Da Capo Press, 1980.

Gourse, Leslie. *Louis' Children.* New York: Quill, 1984.

———. *Madame Jazz.* New York: Oxford University Press, 1995.

Green, Benny. *The Reluctant Art.* New York: Da Capo Press, 1991.

Hadlock, Richard. *Jazz Masters of the '20s.* New York: Da Capo Press, 1972.

Hennessey, Mike. *Klook—The Story of Kenny Clarke.* London, England: Quartet Books Ltd., 1990.

Hentoff, Nat. *The Jazz Life.* New York: Da Capo Press, 1961.

———. *Jazz Is.* New York: Limelight Editions, 1984.

———. *Boston Boy.* New York: Alfred A. Knopf, 1986.

———. *Listen to the Stories.* New York: HarperCollins Publishers, 1995.

Hentoff, Nat, and Albert McCarthy, eds. *Jazz.* New York: Da Capo Press, 1959.

Hilbert, Robert. *Pee Wee Russell.* New York: Oxford University Press, 1993.

Jones, LeRoi (a.k.a. Amiri Baraka). *Black Music.* New York: William Morrow & Co., 1968.

Jones, Max. *Talking Jazz.* New York: W.W. Norton Co., 1988.

Keepnews, Orrin. *The View from Within.* New York: Oxford University Press, 1987.

Lange, Art, and Nathaniel Mackey. *Moment's Notice.* Minneapolis: Coffee House Press, 1993.

Lees, Gene. *Meet Me at Jim & Andy's.* New York: Oxford University Press, 1988.

———. *Jazz, Black & White.* New York: Oxford University Press, 1994.

———. *Leader of the Band—The Life of Woody Herman.* New York: Oxford University Press, 1995.

Maggin, Donald. *Stan Getz—A Life in Jazz.* New York: William Morrow & Co., 1996.

McPartland, Marian. *All in Good Time.* New York: Oxford University Press, 1987.

Mingus, Charles. *Beneath the Underdog.* New York: Alfred A. Knopf, 1971.

Nicholson, Stuart. *Jazz—The 1980s Resurgence.* New York: Da Capo Press, 1995.

Placksin, Sally. *American Women in Jazz.* New York: Wideview Books, 1982.

Porter, Lewis, ed. *A Lester Young Reader.* Washington, D.C.: Smithsonian Institution Press, 1991.

Priestly, Brian. *Mingus.* New York: Da Capo Press, 1982.

Ramsey, Doug. *Jazz Matters.* Fayetteville, Ark.: University of Arkansas Press, 1989.

Roland, Mark, and Tony Scherman. *The Jazz Musician.* New York: St. Martin's Press, 1994.

Rosenthal, David. *Hard Bop.* New York: Oxford University Press, 1992.

Sales, Grover. *Jazz—America's Classical Music.* New York: Da Capo Press, 1992.

Schuller, Gunther. *Early Jazz.* New York: Oxford University Press, 1968.

———. *The Swing Era.* New York: Oxford University Press, 1989.

Shadwick, Keith. *The Illustrated Story of Jazz.* New York: Crescent Books, 1991.

Shapiro, Nat, and Nat Hentoff. *Hear Me Talkin' to Ya.* New York: Dover Publications, 1955.

———. *The Jazz Makers.* New York: Da Capo, 1979.

Shaw, Arnold. *52nd Street.* New York: Da Capo Press, 1971.

Sidran, Ben. *Black Talk.* New York: Da Capo Press, 1971.

———. *Talking Jazz.* New York: Da Capo Press, 1995.

Simon, George. *The Big Bands.* 4th ed. New York: Schirmer Books, 1981.

Stewart, Jimmy. *The Art, History & Style of Jazz Guitar.* Miami, Fla: CPP/Belwin, 1993.

Stewart, Rex. *Jazz Masters of the '30s.* New York: Da Capo Press, 1972.

Taylor, Art. *Notes & Tones.* London, England: Quartet Books Ltd., 1983.

Tucker, Mark. *The Duke Ellington Reader.* New York: Oxford University Press, 1993.

Voce, Steve. *Woody Herman.* London, England: Apollo Press Ltd., 1986.

Williams, Martin. *The Art of Jazz.* New York: Oxford University Press, 1959.

———. *Jazz in Its Time.* New York: Oxford University Press, 1989.

———. *Changes.* New York: Oxford University Press, 1992.

Wilmer, Valerie. *Jazz People.* New York: Da Capo Press, 1977.

———. *Mama Said There'd Be Days Like This.* London, England: The Woman's Press Ltd., 1989.

Wynn, Ron. *All Music Guide to Jazz.* San Francisco: Miller Freeman Books, 1994.

Young, Al. *Things Ain't What They Used To Be.* Berkeley, Calif.: Creative Arts Book Co., 1987.

Discography

The Adderley Brothers. *The Cannonball Adderley Collection,* vols. 1–7. Landmark.

Akiyoshi, Toshiko. *Long Yellow Road.* RCA.

———. *Tales of a Courtesan.* RCA.

Allen, Henry "Red." *Henry "Red" Allen & Coleman Hawkins.* Hep.

———. *World on a String.* RCA Bluebird.

Allison, Mose. *Allison Wonderland.* Rhino.

Ammons, Gene. *All Star Sessions.* OJC.

See also Billie Eckstine and Woody Herman.

Armstrong, Louis. *Hot Fives & Sevens,* vols 1–6 (with Earl Hines). Columbia.

———. *Satchmo and the All Stars at Symphony Hall.* Decca.

Baker, Chet. *Chet.* Riverside.

———. *Complete Pacific Jazz Recordings.* Mosaic.

See also Gerry Mulligan.

Barbieri, Gato. *Latin America.* MCA.

———. *Viva Emiliano Zapata.* GRP.

Basie, Count. *The Complete Decca Recordings.* GRP.

———. *The Complete Roulette Live Recordings.* Mosaic.

———. *The Essential Count Basie,* vols. 1–3. Columbia.

———. *For the First Time.* Pablo.

———. *Rock-a-Bye Basie.* Vintage Jazz.

———. *Satch & Josh* (with Oscar Peterson). Pablo.

———. *Sing Along with Basie* (with Lambert, Hendricks & Ross). Roulette.

———. *Swings with Joe Williams* (live recordings). Polygram.

Bechet, Sidney. *1932–51.* Giants of Jazz.

———. *The Best of Bechet.* Blue Note.

———. *Blues in Thirds* (with Earl Hines). Giants of Jazz.

———. *Complete,* vols. 1–6. RCA.

Beiderbecke, Bix. *Bix & Tram,* vol. 1. JSP.

———. *Bix Beiderbecke,* vols. 1 and 2. Columbia.

Benson, George. *Cook Book.* Columbia.

———. *New Boss Guitar.* OJC.

Berman, Sonny. *Woodchoppers Holiday.* Cool & Blue.

See also Ralph Burns, Serge Chaloff, and Woody Herman.

Blakey, Art. *Art Blakey and the Jazz Messengers.* Impulse.

———. *The History of the Jazz Messengers.* Blue Note.

———. *Kyoto.* Riverside.

———. *A Night at Birdland* (with Clifford Brown). Blue Note.

See also Billy Eckstine and Thelonious Monk.

Bley, Carla. *Fleur Carnivore* (with Lew Soloff and Gary Valente). ECM/Watt.

———. *A Genuine Tong Funeral* (with Gary Burton and Gato Barbieri). RCA.

———. *Very Big Carla Bley Band* (with Lew Soloff and Gary Valente). ECM/Watt.

Brookmeyer, Bob. *Traditionalism Revisited.* World Pacific.

See also Stan Getz, Thad Jones, Gerry Mulligan, Zoot Sims, and Clark Terry.

Brown, Clifford. *Complete Blue Note & Pacific Jazz Recordings.* Mosaic.

———. *Memorial.* OJC.

See also Helen Merrill and Max Roach.

Burns, Ralph. *The Jazz Scene.* Verve.

See also Serge Chaloff, Chubby Jackson, and Woody Herman.

Burrell, Kenny. *Ellington is Forever,* vols. 1 and 2. Fantasy.

———. *Quintet with John Coltrane.* Prestige.

Burton, Gary. *Artist's Choice.* RCA Bluebird.

See also Carla Bley.

Carter, Benny. *Benny Carter, 1929–36.* Classics.

———. *Carter, Gillespie, Inc.* Pablo.

———. *Cosmopolite.* Pablo.

Carter, Betty. *Feel the Fire.* Verve.

Chaloff, Serge. *We the People Bop.* Cool & Blue.

See also Sonny Berman and Woody Herman.

Christian, Charlie. *Edmond Hall.* Classics.

———. *Genius of the Electric Guitar* (with Benny Goodman). Columbia.

———. *Swing to Bop* (with Dizzy Gillespie and Thelonious Monk). Natasha Imports.

Clayton, Buck. *Complete CBS Buck Clayton Jam Sessions.* Mosaic.

See also Count Basie.

Cohn, Al. *Body & Soul* (with Zoot Sims). Muse.

———. *Cohn's Tones.* Savoy.

———. *Motoring Along* (with Zoot Sims). RCA Bluebird.

See also Sonny Berman, Stan Getz, and Woody Herman.

Cole, Nat "King." *Anatomy of a Jam Session* (with Charlie Shavers). Black Lion.

———. *The Keynoters with Nat Cole.* Mercury.

———. *The Verve Story.* Verve.

Coleman, Ornette. *At the Golden Circle.* Blue Note.

Coltrane, John. *Ballads.* Impulse.

———. *Heavyweight Champion.* Rhino/Atlantic.

———. *A Love Supreme.* Impulse.

———. *The Prestige Recordings.* Prestige.

———. *With Johnny Hartman.* Impulse.

See also Kenny Burrell, Miles Davis, and Thelonious Monk.

Corea, Chick. *Now He Sings, Now He Sobs.* Blue Note.

See also Miles Davis and Stan Getz.

Coryell, Larry. *Spaces.* Vanguard.

———. *Tributaries.* Novus.

———. *Twin House* (with Philip Catherine). Atlantic.

See also Gary Burton, Chico Hamilton, Steve Marcus, and Charles Mingus.

Davis, Eddie "Lockjaw." *Afro Jaws.* Riverside.

———. *Very Saxy.* Prestige.

See also Count Basie and Johnny Griffin.

Davis, Miles. *Birth of the Cool* (with Lee Konitz and Gerry Mulligan). Capitol.

———. *The Columbia Years.* Columbia.

———. *Complete Live at the Plugged Nickel.* Columbia.

———. *Filles de Kilimanjaro.* Columbia.

———. *In a Silent Way.* Columbia.

———. *Kind of Blue.* Columbia.

———. *Sketches of Spain.* Columbia.

———. *Walkin'.* Prestige.

Desmond, Paul. *Easy Living* (with Jim Hall). RCA.

———. *With the MJQ.* Red Baron.

See also Jim Hall, Modern Jazz Quartet, and Gerry Mulligan.

Drummond, Ray. *The Essence* (with Hank Jones). DMP Music.

Eager, Allen. *Brothers and Other Mothers.* Savoy.

See also Stan Getz, Gerry Mulligan, Fats Navarro, and Buddy Rich.

Eckstine, Billy. *Mr. B & the Band.* Savoy.

Edison, Harry "Sweets." *Edison's Lights.* Pablo.

See also Count Basie.

Eldridge, Roy. *Just You, Just Me* (with Coleman Hawkins). Stash.

———. *Little Jazz.* Columbia.

———. *Little Jazz: Best of the Verve Years.* Verve.

———. *Roy & Diz.* Verve.

See also Herb Ellis, Coleman Hawkins, Gene Krupa, and Artie Shaw.

Ellington, Duke. *Back to Back* (with Johnny Hodges). Verve.

———. *The Carnegie Hall Concerts 1943–47.* Prestige.

———. *Ellington 1932–41.* Giants of Jazz.

———. *Ellington 1941–51.* Giants of Jazz.

———. *Ellington at Newport.* Columbia.

———. *Ellington at the Whitney.* Impulse.

———. *Ellington with Coleman Hawkins.* Impulse.

———. *Ellington with John Coltrane.* Impulse.

———. *The Great Paris Concert.* Atlantic.

———. *The Jimmy Blanton Era.* Giants of Jazz.

———. *Money Jungle* (with Charles Mingus and Max Roach). Blue Note.

———. *The Okeh Ellington.* Columbia.

———. *The Small Groups.* Columbia.

———. *This One's for Blanton* (with Ray Brown). Pablo.

Ellis, Herb. *Nothing But the Blues* (with Stan Getz and Roy Eldridge). Verve.

See also Stan Getz and Terry Gibbs.

Ervin, Booker. *Setting the Pace* (with Dexter Gordon). Prestige.

See also Charles Mingus.

Evans, Bill. *The Riverside Recordings.* Riverside.

———. *Undercurrent* (with Jim Hall). Blue Note.

See also Miles Davis, Stan Getz, and Lee Konitz.

Evans, Gil. *The Gil Evans Orchestra.* Giants of Jazz.

See also Miles Davis.

Farlow, Tal. *Jazz Masters 41.* Verve.

See also Red Norvo.

Farmer, Art. *Blame It on My Youth.* Contemporary.

———. *Live at the Half Note* (with Jim Hall). Atlantic.

See also Gerry Mulligan.

Ferguson, Maynard. *Dues.* Mainstream.

Fitzgerald, Ella. *Ella at the Opera House, 1958.* Verve.

———. *Lullabies of Birdland.* Decca.

———. *The Songbooks, 1956–64.* Verve.

Getz, Stan. *The Bossa Nova Years* (with Charlie Byrd and Laurindo Almeida). Verve.

———. *The Brothers* (with Z. Sims, A. Eager, B. Moore, and A. Cohn). Prestige.

———. *Captain Marvel* (with Chick Corea). Columbia.

———. *Diz & Getz.* Verve.

———. *Gold* (with JoAnne Brackeen). Inner City.

———. *Live at Storyville with Jimmy Raney.* Giants of Jazz.

———. *Move, Birdland 1952–3* (with Jimmy Raney). Natasha Imports.

———. *Nobody Else But Me* (with Gary Burton). Verve.

———. *People Time* (with Kenny Barron). Verve.

———. *Quartet & Quintet, 1950–52.* Giants of Jazz.

———. *Stan Getz & Bill Evans.* Verve.

———. *Stan Getz & J.J. Johnson at the Opera House.* Verve.

———. *With the Oscar Peterson Trio.* Verve.

See also Lionel Hampton, Woody Herman, and Abbey Lincoln.

Gibbs, Terry. *Dream Band,* vols. 1–5. Contemporary.

———. *Memories of You* (with Herb Ellis and Milt Hinton). Contemporary.

See also Woody Herman and Chubby Jackson.

Gillespie, Dizzy. *Birk's Works* (big band with Lee Morgan and Melba Liston). Verve.

———. *Compact Jazz.* Mercury.

———. *The Complete RCA Victor Recordings.* RCA Bluebird.

———. *Copenhagen Concert.* Steeple Chase.

———. *Development of an American Artist.* Smithsonian Recordings.

———. *Dizzy's Diamonds.* Verve.

———. *Gillespiana* (with Lalo Schiffren). Verve.

———. *Groovin' High.* Savoy.

———. *Max + Diz, Paris 1989.* A&M.

———. *On the Riviera.* Phillips.

———. *Portrait of Duke Ellington.* Verve.

———. *Sonny Side Up* (with Sonny Rollins and Sonny Stitt). Verve.

———. *Swing Low Sweet Cadillac.* Impulse.

———. *With Stuff Smith.* Verve.

See also Stan Getz, Coleman Hawkins, Red Norvo, and Charlie Parker.

Giuffre, Jimmy. *In Hollywood & Newport* (with Jim Hall and Bob Brookmeyer). Fresh Sound.

———. *Jimmy Giuffre 3.* Atlantic.

See also Bob Brookmeyer and Woody Herman.

Goodman, Benny. *Benny: On the Air, 1937–8.* Columbia.

———. *The Carnegie Hall Concert—1937.* Columbia.

———. *Small Combos 1935–41.* Giants of Jazz.

See also Charlie Christian.

Gordon, Dexter. *Dexter's Mood* (with Melba Liston). Cool & Blue.

———. *More Power.* Prestige.

See also Billy Eckstine and Booker Ervin.

Green, Grant. *Complete Blue Note Recordings.* Mosaic.

Griffin, Johnny. *Introducing Johnny Griffin.* Blue Note.

———. *Tough Tenors* (with Lockjaw Davis). Jazzland.

See also Thelonious Monk.

Hall, Jim. *Concierto* (with Chet Baker and Paul Desmond). Verve.

———. *Dialogues.* Telarc.

See also Jimmy Guiffre, Chico Hamilton, John Lewis, and Sonny Rollins.

Hamilton, Chico. *The Dealer* (with Larry Coryell). Impulse.

———. *Gongs East* (with Eric Dolphy). Discovery.

———. *Passin' Thru* (with Charles Lloyd and Gabor Szabo). Impulse.

———. *Quintet* (with Jim Hall). Pacific Jazz.

See also John Lewis and Gerry Mulligan.

Hampton, Lionel. *Gene Norman Presents Just Jazz.* MCA.

———. *Hamp & Getz.* Verve.

———. *Hot Mallets.* RCA Bluebird.

———. *Vintage Hampton.* Telarc.

See also Charlie Christian and Benny Goodman.

Hampton, Slide. *The JazzMasters/ Dedicated to Diz.* Telarc.

Hartman, Johnny. *Unforgettable.* Impulse.

See also John Coltrane.

Hawkins, Coleman. *At the Opera House with Roy Eldridge.* Verve.

———. *Classic Tenors* (with Lester Young). Signature.

———. *Encounters Ben Webster.* Verve.

———. *Hollywood Stampede* (with Howard McGee). Capitol.

———. *Rainbow Mist* (with Dizzy Gillespie). Delmark.

———. *A Retrospective, 1929–63.* RCA Bluebird.

See also Red Allen, Roy Eldridge, Max Roach, and Sonny Rollins.

Haynes, Roy. *Out of the Afternoon* (with Rahsaan Roland Kirk). Impulse.

See also Charlie Parker.

Henderson, Joe. *Lush Life.* Verve.

———. *The Milestone Years.* Milestone.

Hendricks, Jon. *The Freddie Freeloader Sessions.* Denon.

Herman, Woody. *At Carnegie Hall—1946.* Verve/MetroJazz.

———. *Compact Jazz.* Verve.

———. *The Concord Years* (with Stan Getz and Dizzy Gillespie). Concord.

———. *The First Herd.* Charly.

———. *40th Anniversary Concert.* RCA Bluebird.

———. *Giant Steps.* OJC.

———. *Jazz Masters 54.* Verve.

———. *Keeper of the Flame.* Capitol.

———. *New Directions—Small Groups.* Columbia.

———. *The Thundering Herds.* Columbia.

———. *The V-Disc Years.* Hep.

———. *The Wildroot Broadcasts.* Artistry.

———. *With Charlie Parker, 1951.* Drive Archive.

———. *Woody's Winners.* Columbia.

See also Sonny Berman, Ralph Burns, Serge Chaloff, and Chubby Jackson.

Hill, Andrew. *Faces of Hope.* Soul Note.

———. *Point of Departure* (with Eric Dolphy). Capitol.

See also Sam Rivers.

Hines, Earl. *The Hines Orchestra, 1941.* Classics.

———. *The Legendary Little Theater Concert, 1964.* Muse.

———. *Partners in Jazz* (with Jaki Byard). MPS.

———. *Piano Man.* RCA Bluebird.

———. *Up to Date* (with Budd Johnson). RCA Bluebird.

See also Louis Armstrong and Sidney Bechet.

Hinton, Milt. *Branford Marsalis—Trio Jeepy.* Columbia.

———. *Old Man Time.* Chiaroscuro.

Hodges, Johnny. *Passion Flower.* RCA Bluebird.

———. *Used to be Duke.* Verve.

See also Duke Ellington.

Holiday, Billie. *The Quintessential Billie Holiday* (with Lester Young). Columbia.

Ibriham, Abdullah. *Ekaya.* Enja.

———. *Ode to Duke Ellington.* Westwind.

Jackie & Roy. *Charlie Ventura Pasedena Concert.* GNP.

———. *High Standards.* Concord.

———. *Jackie & Roy.* Savoy.

Jackson, Chubby. *Big Band with Gerry Mulligan.* OJC.

———. *Chubby's Back.* Argo.

———. *The Happy Monster* (with Conte Candoli, Bill Harris, and Terry Gibbs). Cool & Blue.

See also Woody Herman.

Jackson, Milt. *In the Beginning.* OJC.

———. *Live at the Village Gate.* OJC.

———. *Mostly Duke.* Pablo.

———. *Opus de Jazz.* Savoy.

See also Dizzy Gillespie, Modern Jazz Quartet, and Wes Montgomery.

Jacquet, Illinois. *The Big Band—Jacquet's Got It.* Atlantic.

———. *Flying Home.* Verve.

———. *The King.* OJC.

———. *The Verve Story.* Verve.

Jarrett, Keith. *At the Blue Note.* ECM.

———. *Foundations.* Rhino.

See also Charles Lloyd.

Johnson, Budd. *With the Four Brass Giants.* OJC.

See also Earl Hines and Nat Cole.

Johnson, J.J. *Trombone by Three.* OJC.

See also Stan Getz and Sonny Stitt.

Jones, Thad, and Mel Lewis. *The Complete Solid State Recordings* (with Bob Brookmeyer). Mosaic.

Jordan, Sheila. *George Russell—The Outer View.* OJC.

———. *Lost & Found.* Muse.

———. *Portrait of Sheila.* Blue Note.

Kenton, Stan. *Complete Capitol Recordings of Bill Holman & Bill Russo Charts.* Mosaic.

———. *Intermission Riff, 1952–6.* Giants of Jazz.

———. *New Concepts.* Capitol.

Kirk, Rahsaan Roland. *Does Your House Have Lions.* Rhino.

———. *Kirk's Works.* OJC.

———. *Left & Right.* Atlantic.

See also Roy Haynes and Charles Mingus.

Konitz, Lee. *First Sessions.* Prestige.

———. *Live at the Half Note* (with Bill Evans). Verve.

———. *Meets Gerry Mulligan.* Capitol.

See also Miles Davis and Claude Thornhill.

Krupa, Gene. *Uptown* (with Roy Eldridge and Anita O'Day). CBS.

Lambert, Dave. *Early Bebop* (with Buddy Stewart). Mercury.

Lambert, Hendricks & Ross. *Everybody's Boppin'.* Columbia.

———. *Sing a Song of Basie.* Impulse.

See also Count Basie.

Lateef, Yusef. *Every Village Has a Song.* Rhino.

See also The Adderly Brothers.

Lewis, John. *Grand Encounter* (with Jim Hall and Bill Perkins). Capitol.

See also Dizzy Gillespie and Modern Jazz Quartet.

Lincoln, Abbey. *Straight Ahead.* Blue Note.

———. *You Gotta Pay the Band* (with Stan Getz). Verve.

See also Max Roach.

Liston, Melba. *And Her Bones.* MetroJazz.

See also Dizzy Gillespie, Dexter Gordon, and Randy Weston.

Lloyd, Charles. *Forest Flower.* Atlantic.

———. *Of Course, Of Course.* Columbia.

See also Chico Hamilton and The Adderley Brothers.

Machito. *The Original Mambo Kings* (with Charlie Parker and Dizzy Gillespie). Verve.

Marcus, Steve. *Count's Rock Band* (with Larry Coryell). Vortex/Atlantic.

———. *Tomorrow* (with Larry Coryell). Vortex/Atlantic.

Marsalis, Wynton. *Standard Time,* vol. 1. Columbia.

See also Art Blakey.

McConnell, Rob. *Live in Digital.* Sea Breeze.

McRae, Carmen. *Any Old Time.* Denon.

———. *Carman Sings Monk.* Novus.

McShann, Jay. *Blues From Kansas City* (with Charlie Parker). Decca.

Merrill, Helen. *Brownie—An Homage to Clifford Brown.* Verve.

———. *A Shade of Difference.* Landmark.

———. *With Clifford Brown.* PolyGram.

Mingus, Charles. *The Black Saint & the Sinner Lady* (with Charlie Mariano). Impulse.

———. *Complete 1959 CBS Sessions.* Mosaic.

———. *Epitaph.* Columbia.

———. *Goodbye Pork Pie Hat.* Jazz Hour.

———. *Gunslinging Birds—The Mingus Big Band.* Dreyfus.

———. *Mingus in Europe.* Enja.

———. *Nostalgia in Times Square—The Mingus Big Band.* Dreyfus.

———. *Presents Charles Mingus* (with Eric Dolphy). Candid.

———. *Thirteen Pictures.* Rhino.

See also Duke Ellington and Red Norvo.

Modern Jazz Quartet. *Concorde.* Prestige.

———. *Django.* Prestige.

———. *The Last Concert.* Rhino.

———. *MJQ—40 Years.* Atlantic.

See also Milt Jackson and John Lewis.

Monk, Thelonious. *Big Band & Quartet in Concert.* Columbia.

———. *The Blue Note Years.* Blue Note.

———. *Complete Riverside Recordings.* Riverside.

———. *Live at Newport, 1958 & 1963* (with Pee Wee Russell). Columbia.

———. *Monk's Dream.* Columbia.

———. *Standards.* Columbia.

Montgomery, Wes. *Complete Riverside Recordings.* Riverside.

———. *The Verve Jazz Sides.* Verve.

Moore, Brew. *I Should Care.* Steeple Chase.

See also Stan Getz and Kai Winding.

Morgan, Lee. *The Sidewinder.* Blue Note.

See also Art Blakey and Dizzy Gillespie.

Moss, Ann Marie. *Two for the Road.* Stash.

Mulligan, Gerry. *Concert Jazz Band, Paris Jazz Concert* (with Zoot Sims). Europe 1.

———. *Meets Ben Webster.* PolyGram.

———. *Meets Stan Getz.* Verve.

———. *Meets the Saxophonists.* PolyGram.

———. *Pacific Jazz & Capitol Recordings* (with Chet Baker and Bob Brookmeyer). Mosaic.

———. *Plays Mulligan* (with Allen Eager). OJC.

———. *Quartet & with Chubby Jackson's Big Band.* OJC.

———. *What Is There to Say* (with Art Farmer). Columbia.

See also Miles Davis, Lee Konitz, and Kai Winding.

Navarro, Fats. *Fats Blows, 1946–49* (with Allen Eager). Fresh Sound.

———. *In the Beginning Bebop.* Savoy.

———. *Royal Roost Sessions* (with Allen Eager). Fresh Sound.

———. *With Tadd Dameron* (with Allen Eager). Milestone.

Neidlinger, Buell. *Buellgrass.* K2B2.

———. *Locomotive.* Soul Note.

See also Cecil Taylor.

Norvo, Red. *Fabulous Jam Session* (with Dizzy Gillespie and Charlie Parker). Stash.

———. *The Savoy Sessions* (with Charles Mingus and Tal Farlow). Savoy.

See also Woody Herman.

O'Day, Anita. *Tea for Two.* Moon.

See also Gene Krupa.

Paris, Jackie. *Jackie Paris.* Audiophile.

———. *Lucky to Be Me.* Emarcy.

See also Charles Mingus.

Parker, Charlie. *Bird & Fats at Birdland.* Cool & Blue.

———. *The Complete Dial Sessions.* Stash.

———. *From Dizzy to Miles.* Giants of Jazz.

———. *Jazz at Massey Hall.* OJC.

———. *Jazz Masters 15.* Verve.

See also Dizzy Gillespie, Woody Herman, Machito, Jay McShann, and Red Norvo.

Perkins, Bill. *On Stage.* Pacific Jazz.

———. *With the Metropole Orchestra.* Candid.

See also Woody Herman, Stan Kenton, and John Lewis.

Pomeroy, Herb. *Band in Boston.* Roulette.

———. *Big Band Renaissance.* Smithsonian Recordings.

Powell, Bud. *The Amazing Bud Powell,* vols. 1 and 2. Blue Note.

See also Sonny Stitt.

Raeburn, Boyd. *Boyd Meets Stravinsky* (with Dizzy Gillespie). Savoy.

Raney, Jimmy. *The Complete Jimmy Raney in Tokyo.* Xanadu.

———. *Jimmy & Doug Raney Quartet.* Steeple Chase.

———. *Two Jims & Zoot* (with Jim Hall and Zoot Sims). Mainstream.

See also Stan Getz and Zoot Sims.

Redmond, Joshua. *Wish.* Warner.

Reinhardt, Django. *Jazz Masters 38.* Verve.

———. *Swing in Paris.* Affinity.

Rich, Buddy. *Best Band I Ever Had.* DCC.

———. *His Legendary Orchestra, 1947–8* (with Allen Eager). Hep.

———. *Live at Ronnie Scott's.* DRG.

Rivers, Sam. *Involution* (with Andrew Hill). Blue Note.

Roach, Max. *Alone Together* (with Clifford Brown). Verve.

———. *Deeds Not Words.* Riverside.

———. *Max Roach + 4.* Emarcy.

———. *M'Boom.* Columbia.

———. *To the Max.* Blue Moon.

———. *We Insist!—Freedom Now Suite.* Candid.

See also Dizzy Gillespie, Coleman Hawkins, Abbey Lincoln, Charlie Parker, and Sonny Rollins.

Rollins, Sonny. *All the Things You Are* (with Coleman Hawkins). RCA Bluebird.

———. *The Bridge* (with Jim Hall). RCA Bluebird.

———. *The Complete Prestige Recordings.* Prestige.

———. *Don't Stop the Carnival.* Milestone.

———. *Freedom Suite.* Riverside.

———. *Way Out West.* Contemporary.

Ross, Annie. *Annie Ross Sings with Mulligan.* Pacific Jazz.

———. *The Gasser.* (with Zoot Sims). Pacific Jazz.

Rouse, Charlie. *Epistrophy.* Landmark.

———. *Unsung Hero.* Columbia.

See also Thelonious Monk.

Rushing, Jimmy. *The Essential Jimmy Rushing.* Vanguard.

See also Count Basie.

Russell, Pee Wee. *Ask Me Now.* Impulse.

———. *Jazz Reunion.* Candid.

———. *With Jack Teagarden.* OJC.

See also Thelonious Monk.

Schneider, Maria. *Evanescance.* Enja.

Shaw, Artie. *The Complete Artie Shaw,* vol. 7 (with Roy Eldridge). RCA.

———. *The Gramercy Five Sessions* (with Roy Eldridge and Barney Kessel). RCA Bluebird.

Sheldon, Jack. *On My Own.* Concord.

Shepp, Archie. *Four for Trane.* Impulse.

———. *Goin' Home.* Steeple Chase.

———. *Trouble in Mind.* Steeple Chase.

Silver, Horace. *Doin' the Thing.* Blue Note.

———. *Song for My Father.* Blue Note.

———. *Sterling Silver.* Blue Note.

See also Art Blakey and Stan Getz.

Simone, Nina. *After Hours.* Verve.

———. *My Baby Just Cares for Me.* Happy Days.

Sims, Zoot. *And the Gershwin Brothers.* OJC.

———. *Morning Fun* (with Bob Brookmeyer). Black Lion.

———. *Quartets.* OJC.

———. *The Swinger.* OJC.

———. *With Count Basie.* Pablo.

See also Stan Getz, Woody Herman, and Gerry Mulligan.

Steig, Jeremy. *Jeremy & the Satyrs.* Reprise.

———. *Outlaws* (with Eddie Gomez). Enja.

Stitt, Sonny. *With Bud Powell & J.J. Johnson.* OJC.

———. *With the Oscar Peterson Trio.* Verve.

See also Gene Ammons and Dizzy Gillespie.

Szabo, Gabor. *Gypsy '66.* Impulse.

———. *The Sorcerer.* Impulse.

———. *Spellbinder.* Impulse.

See also Chico Hamilton and Charles Lloyd.

Terry, Clark. *Gingerbread* (with Bob Brookmeyer). Mainstream.

See also Count Basie, Duke Ellington, and Thelonious Monk.

Thornhill, Claude. *The Uncollected Recordings.* Hindsight.

Timmons, Bobby. *In Person.* OJC.

See also The Adderly Brothers.

Various. *The Bebop Era.* Columbia.

Various. *Big Band Jazz—The Beginnings to the '50s.* Smithsonian Recordings.

Various. *Big Band Renaissance—The 1940s and Beyond.* Smithsonian Recordings.

Various. *Classic Jazz.* Smithsonian Recordings.

Various. *The Complete Commodore Jazz Recordings.* Mosaic.

Various. *The Esquire Jazz Concert—1944.* Giants of Jazz.

Various. *Great Trumpets.* RCA Bluebird.

Various. *JATP—the First Concerts.* Verve.

Various. *Jazz Piano.* Smithsonian Recordings.

Various. *The Jazz Scene.* Verve.

Various. *Legends of Jazz Guitar.* Rhino.

Various. *The Verve Story.* Verve.

Vax, Mike. *Trumpets.* Jazz Alliance.

Weather Report. *Black Market.* Columbia.

———. *8:30.* Columbia.

———. *Heavy Weather.* Columbia.

———. *I Sing the Body Electric.* Columbia.

———. *Night Passage.* Columbia.

———. *Weather Report.* Columbia.

Webster, Ben. *The Frog.* Giants of Jazz.

———. *Jazz Masters 43.* Verve.

———. *Soulmates.* OJC.

———. *The Soul of Ben Webster.* Verve.

See also Duke Ellington, Coleman Hawkins, and Gerry Mulligan.

Weston, Randy. *Portraits of Duke Ellington.* Verve.

———. *Portraits of Thelonious Monk.* Verve.

———. *Spirits of Our Ancestors* (with Melba Liston's arrangements). Antilles.

———. *Volcano Blues* (with Melba Liston's arrangements). Antilles.

Williams, Cootie. *Introduction, 1930–43.* Best of Jazz.

See also Charlie Christian, Duke Ellington, and Benny Goodman.

Williams, Joe. *Live.* OJC.

———. *Live at Century Plaza with the Capp-Pierce Juggernaut.* Concord.

See also Count Basie.

Williams, Tony. *Lifetime Emergency.* Polydor.

———. *Tokyo Live.* Blue Note.

See also Miles Davis.

Winding, Kai. *Bop City* (with Gerry Mulligan and Brew Moore). Cool & Blue.

Young, Lester. *And the Piano Giants.* Verve.

———. *Complete Aladdin Recordings.* Blue Note.

———. *Complete Keynote Recordings.* Mercury.

———. *Complete Savoy Recordings.* Savoy.

———. *The Lester Young Story.* Columbia.

———. *Prez & Friends.* Commodore.

———. *Trio with Nat Cole & Buddy Rich.* Verve.

See also Count Basie and Billie Holiday.

Index